TRULY ITALIAN

TRULY ITALIAN

URSULA FERRIGNO

MITCHELL BEAZLEY

DEDICATION

I would like to dedicate this book to
Limelight Management, for all they do
for me; to my very good friend Wendy
Fogarty, who has been so supportive of
all my projects; to all at Books for Cooks,
especially Eric Treiulle and Rosie; and
finally to my family.

TRULY ITALIAN
by Ursula Ferrigno

First published in Great Britain in 1999
by Mitchell Beazley, an imprint of
Octopus Publishing Group Ltd
2–4 Heron Quays, London E14 4JP

Reprinted 2000

ISBN 1 84000 149 6

A CIP catalogue record for this book is
available from the British Library.
The author and publisher will be grateful
for any information that will assist them
in keeping future editions up to date.
Although all reasonable care has been
taken in the preparation of this book,
neither the publisher nor the author can
accept liablility for any consequences
arising from the use thereof, or from the
information contained therein.

Commissioning Editor: Margaret Little
Art Director: Gaye Allen
Editors: Susan Fleming and
Margot Richardson
Production: Karen Farquhar
Index: Angie Hipkin

Typeset in New Caledonia and Trajan
Printed and bound by Toppan Printing
Company in China.

CONTENTS

AN
ITALIAN KITCHEN

WHENEVER I TRAVEL IN ITALY I am surrounded by food, from the colour-ful, boisterous fruit and vegetable markets and small specialist shops tucked into winding streets, to quiet, reflective places like art galleries in Milan, and churches and cathedrals, with paintings such as da Vinci's *Cenacolo* or 'Last Supper', depicting a humble meal of bread and wine. Near Siena, at the monastery of Monte Oliveto Maggiore, a beautiful Della Robbia wreath of realistic-looking fruits, vines and flowers welcomes visitors to the serenity of the building and its surrounding landscape. Painted flowers, breads and fruits abound on the walls of the Uffizi Art Gallery in Florence.

I am as enamoured of Italian food as the artists were who depicted it so many centuries ago. Like them, I admire its simplicity and its symbolism, and whatever I cook, there is usually a story connecting the dish I am preparing with some aspect of its history. My grandmother, from whom I learned so much about food, used to entertain me for hours with her stories of the families at home in our village of Minori: they were all laden with references to individual anniversaries, to festivals held to mark some part of the religious calendar, or to celebrations to acknowledge the seasonal arrival of one of the local foods.

To learn about Italian food is to understand Italian people – their respect for food and the role that it has played in their history. For to Italians, food represents more than satisfying hunger: it is the focal point of their lives and their traditions, whether it is *torta pasqualina* (Easter pie made with thirty layers of pastry to commemorate the years of Christ's life), *ossi dei morti* ('bones of the dead' biscuits made in memory of deceased relatives), or a chestnut soup made in autumn with the newly harvested nuts, and gilded with a sprinkling of new olive oil, freshly pressed from the abundant fruit. Italian food encapsulates history, tradition and folklore, plus an acute and unique awareness of nature and seasonality, which truly provides 'food for thought'.

My family come from the south of Italy, and because our natural daily diet was so rich in the local vegetables, I learned to prefer eating meals that did not include meat. In fact, it is true to say that most Italians eat a diet that is more vegetarian in essence than that of most other nations in Europe. With the accessibility of a myriad varieties of pastas and pulses, of rice, and the huge abundance of vegetables and fruit, meat plays a distinctly secondary role in daily life and eating. When it *is* enjoyed, it is usually in quite small quantities, as an afterthought almost: a pasta or fresh vegetable dish is still, to many Italians, the most important intake of the day!

And, of course, because of agricultural tradition, most of the farmland in Italy is given over to vegetable and cereal production rather than to cattle or sheep grazing. And because the majority of this production is small, intimate and organic, with little commerce involved, the farmers are uniquely allied to their land and their produce, with an inherent knowledge of how to nourish the soil and cherish the plants. They sow carefully, grow carefully and harvest carefully, and all this results in what I think are the best vegetables, grains and fruits in the world.

A diet consisting principally of vegetables, grains and fruits, with the addition of seeds and nuts, is an extremely healthy one, attested to by the recent acclamation given to the 'Mediterranean Diet' by doctors and other health professionals. Italian food illustrates *par excellence* the 'principles' of this way of eating: an emphasis on carbohydrates such as vegetables, pulses, grains – and the foods made with them, such as bread and pasta – fruits, seeds and nuts; a lesser intake of protein in the form of meat and dairy products; plus a wide usage of the major unifying factor of the whole of the Mediterranean area: our magnificent olive oil.

The essential elements of diet in general are carbohydrate (and fibre), protein and fat. Carbohydrate, which consists of sugars and starches, is the main fuel of the body, and it is amply supplied in the Italian diet, and in a vegetarian diet. It comes

in two forms, which are generally called 'fast-release' and 'slow-release'. The former are foods such as sugars, cakes, sweets and many refined products, and they give a quick boost of energy to the body's blood sugar levels; these levels soon slump down again, though, which is undesirable. Slow-release or complex carbohydrates give more sustained and valuable energy to the body, as their sugars are, literally, released more slowly into the bloodstream. These foods include vegetables, fruit and grains, and you can then understand how a lunch of a vegetable and pasta dish can see you happily throughout the afternoon. Fibre consists of the parts of vegetables that the human gut cannot digest, and a good intake of it is necessary for effective metabolism; it is also protective against many diseases.

Amino acids are the building blocks of protein, and many need to be provided in the diet. 'Complete' proteins contain all the amino acids necessary for the body, and complete protein foods are meats, dairy products and soya beans (the only one of non-animal origin). Other protein foods are grains, pulses, nuts and seeds, but they do not contain *all* the essential amino acids, so are known as 'incomplete' proteins. However, nature has cleverly arranged that a combination of a complete and incomplete protein – such as egg or cheese with bread, or cheese with pasta – or a grain with pulses and/or nuts (rice with beans, for instance), can provide almost as much necessary protein as expensively reared meat.

9

Meat also contains a great deal of fat, which is saturated and therefore potentially damaging to the body. We need to have some fat intake, but we should choose in preference polyunsaturated fats that are part of the structure of seeds, nuts and grains, and, for vegetarians, the fats contained in animal by-products such as milk, cheese and eggs. But the supreme health of the peoples who live around the Mediterranean has been directly linked to the glories of olive oil, a monounsaturated fat that actually contributes positively to health. Fat makes food more palatable, and olive oil is the perfect answer.

Also necessary are vitamins and minerals, needed for continuing good health. Fresh raw foods and carefully cooked foods will provide all that you need, and in the *Consiglio* – the tip or piece of advice – at the bottom of many recipes, I have pointed out a particular benefit of an ingredient, whether it be the Vitamin A contained in yellow pumpkin flesh or the digestive property of fennel seeds.

I have always enjoyed telling my students about the closing of all business activity in Italy between the hours of 1 and 4 pm. Everyone rushes home to enjoy the main meal of the day; the traffic becomes even more furious than usual and tempers rise as hunger grows. The silent streets thereafter indicate that behind closed doors the very important business of eating, enjoying and unifying the family has begun.

An Italian meal follows a strict pattern, and consists of many courses. First, there are *antipasti*, a mere taste of something delicious, or a *minestra*, soup. Then there is the *primo piatto*, the first course, which is pasta, risotto or polenta. The *secondo piatto* is generally the meat or fish course, usually very small, served entirely by itself. This is followed by the *contorno*, vegetable course, then – at least certainly in our family – an *insalata* or salad. A piece of fresh fruit would be all that most people would have thereafter, or simply a coffee. Cakes and biscuits are for eating with coffee in the morning or afternoon rather than after a meal. Because of this emphasis on foods and dishes following each other rather than being served all at once, the individual flavours of foods and dishes can be so much more recognised and appreciated – one of the aspects I most love about Italian food.

I do urge you to try and eat in this Italian way. It will be a revelation, as I hope this book will be. Although it consists mostly of traditional everyday Italian recipes, none of them requires any special skills, or hours of hard labour in the kitchen (apart from the breads, but that is different!). They are simple and straightforward, and are also extremely colourful, tasty and satisfying. I wish you, your family and all your friends great joy with these dishes.

Ursula Ferrigno

PASTA

Pasta is an ancient food, and cave drawings in Imperia, northern Italy, suggest that it was around long before Marco Polo was said to have brought it from China.

Pasta is fundamental to Italian life, and my uncle once said, 'A meal without pasta isn't a proper meal'. It is a daily ritual, consumed every lunch or dinner time as part of the first course, *primo piatto*, and never as a whole meal on its own. It was once a southern speciality (in the north they favoured rice and polenta), but pasta has somehow united Italy, and it is now eaten the length and breadth of the country. During the Renaissance, pasta – especially lasagne, ravioli and tortellini – was found only on the tables of the wealthy. In the nineteenth century, though, it came to be viewed as food for the poor, especially in Naples. This century, Mussolini went so far as to consider banning it from the Italian diet because he thought it made the army lethargic!

Fresh pasta is delicious, if time consuming to make, but most dried pastas are of very good quality and are preferable to the frozen fresh pastas available. I have not given timings in the following recipes as the packet instructions will be more precise: the number of minutes involved will depend on the shape and thickness of the pasta. The pasta is ready when it is tender but with a central resistance to the bite: *al dente*. The water must always be salted, and at a rolling boil. The sauce you choose will also depend on the pasta's shape and thickness: thin and long pasta suits an oily, more liquid sauce; more complicated shapes will have holes and curves in which a thicker sauce can nestle and cling. In fact, almost as regularly as in Italian fashion shows, a new pasta seems to appear which has been specifically designed to enhance the 'cling' effect.

Freshly grated Parmesan cheese is sprinkled on to most pasta dishes, enhancing their nutritional benefits with its added protein and calcium. It is not, however, added to most mushroom pasta dishes (nor to fish pastas or risottos).

I eat pasta daily; it's the only thing that I know I will definitely do each day. One's imagination can run riot with ingredients for a pasta sauce: you can use a myriad of vegetables, pulses, cheeses, oils, herbs and spices. Most of the recipes here use the simple pastas – spaghetti and tagliatelle – which are most often used at home, *a casa*, in Italy. This saves having many half-used packets of different shapes cluttering up your cupboards.

I do hope you will enjoy the following selection of my all-time favourite, healthy pasta recipes.

PASTA E FAGIOLI
Pasta and Beans

This famous soup-meal must, according to my grandmother, be served hot with a 'C' trickled over the surface in olive oil. Foolishly, I never found out why! The original recipe advises cooking the beans in an earthenware pot in a slow oven for three hours. I find, however, that excellent results are obtained if the recipe is streamlined and adapted to modern rhythms: cooked and ready to serve in an hour and a half. Italian soups are not as liquid as those elsewhere, so don't worry if it looks too thick.

SERVES 6

300g (11 oz) dried cannellini beans, or 2 x 400g (14 oz) cans cooked beans
1 sprig fresh sage
1 sprig fresh rosemary
2 garlic cloves, peeled and crushed
sea salt and freshly ground black pepper

dried chilli-pepper flakes to taste
200g (7 oz) rigatoni (short, ribbed noodles)
extra virgin olive oil
freshly grated Parmesan to taste

1 Soak the dried beans in water for 24 hours. Drain, cover with fresh water and a lid, and bring to the boil for 10 minutes. Thereafter, cook over a gentle heat for 40 minutes, along with the herbs and garlic to lend flavour and aroma.

2 If using canned beans, simply drain and rinse, add the herbs and garlic, then just cover with cold water and heat through for about 20 minutes. Top up with more water as necessary.

3 Push the beans and liquid through a sieve to eliminate the tough outer husks, then place the purée in a saucepan. Season with salt and pepper and a little chilli to taste.

4 Cook the pasta in the bean purée, stirring occasionally to prevent the pasta sticking. Add a little water, about 4 tablespoons, to finish cooking.

5 To serve, drizzle the hot soup with extra virgin olive oil and sprinkle with Parmesan to taste.

A high-carbohydrate and high-energy dish, perfect for winter especially – and it uses virtually no oil. Other pulses could be used in this recipe in place of the cannellini beans. It's so potentially versatile, you'll soon be able to put your own stamp on the recipe.

TAGLIATELLE AL MASCARPONE E SPINACI

Tagliatelle with Mascarpone and Spinach

In Italy, spinach is available in delicatessens, cooked and prepared, squashed and squeezed into a ball ready to take home and dress simply with oil and lemon – the very best way of serving cold cooked vegetables.

SERVES 4

20 g (¾ oz) butter
1 garlic clove, peeled and
**   left whole**
300 g (11 oz) fresh spinach
**   leaves, washed and finely**
**   chopped**
150 ml (¼ pint) double cream

150 g (5 oz) Mascarpone cheese
275 g (10 oz) tagliatelle
**   (ribbon noodles)**
sea salt and freshly ground
**   black pepper**
freshly grated nutmeg

1 Melt the butter, add the whole garlic, and cook gently, allowing the garlic to turn golden brown, but taking care not to burn the butter.

2 Add the finely chopped spinach and cook over a low heat until tender, a few minutes only.

3 In a separate pan, simmer the cream and Mascarpone together gently for a few minutes.

4 Cook the pasta in plenty of rolling, boiling salted water until *al dente*. Drain well and turn into a warm serving bowl.

5 Add first the cream sauce, and then the spinach, having removed the garlic. Season with salt, pepper and nutmeg and mix well. Serve at once.

Spinach is rich in iron and Vitamins A, E and C. It's known as the 'international king of vegetables', and is said to prevent many ailments. I particularly love young tender spinach leaves, and like to eat them raw in a salad.

TAGLIATELLE AI CARCIOFI

Tagliatelle with Artichokes

Mint and artichokes are great in combination, having a natural affinity with each other. This is a good recipe to treat yourself to during the artichoke season which, in Italy, is April, May and October.

SERVES 4

4 globe artichokes
2 tablespoons olive oil
25 g (1 oz) unsalted butter
1 small onion, peeled
  and chopped
150 ml (¼ pint) dry white wine
juice of 1 lemon
150 ml (¼ pint) home-made
  vegetable stock (*see* page 61)

275 g (10 oz) tagliatelle
  (ribbon noodles)
200 ml (7 fl oz) double cream
a handful of fresh mint,
  chopped
sea salt and freshly ground
  black pepper
55 g (2 oz) freshly grated
  Parmesan

1 Prepare the artichokes by removing the tough outer leaves, and cutting off the spiky, pointed top. Remove the stalk and cut each vegetable lengthways into 8 segments. Cut away the prickly choke and discard any tough leaves that might spoil the sauce. Put the artichoke segments into water with a little vinegar or extra lemon juice to prevent discoloration. Just before using them, drain and chop.

2 Heat the oil and butter in a large saucepan, and gently fry the chopped onion until soft. Keep the heat low and cover the pan. After about 5 minutes add the chopped artichoke. Stir, cover again and cook for another

5 minutes. Add the white wine, lemon juice and vegetable stock. Cook gently, covered, for 15 minutes.

3 Meanwhile, heat the water for the pasta. Once you have added the pasta to the rolling, boiling, salted water, stir the cream and mint into the artichoke mixture and leave uncovered on a very low heat. Season with salt and pepper. The sauce will become thick while the pasta is cooking.

4 Drain the pasta when it is *al dente*, and immediately stir in the freshly grated Parmesan so that all the pasta is coated with the cheese. Now pour on the artichoke sauce and stir vigorously. Serve at once.

Artichokes contain cynarine, an enzyme which is said to be liver protective, to be good for the kidneys and to lower blood cholesterol. Cynarine also makes everything in your mouth taste quite sweet, so you should never try to drink a good wine with artichokes.

TAGLIATELLE ALLA BOSCAIOLA
Tagliatelle 'of the Forest'

Italians love wild mushrooms, which grow all over the country in damp, cool forests. The most common wild mushroom is the *porcino*, penny bun or cep (*Boletus edulis*). It is often dried, which makes the flavour intensify and deepen. You can replace half the mushrooms here with 55g (2oz) dried *porcini*: soak them in cold water first for about ten minutes.

SERVES 4

3 tablespoons olive oil

2 garlic cloves, peeled and finely chopped

1 x 400g (14oz) can Italian plum tomatoes

sea salt and freshly ground black pepper

275g (10oz) fresh wild or field mushrooms, wiped and finely diced

a handful of fresh flat-leaf parsley, chopped

275g (10oz) tagliatelle (ribbon noodles)

1 Heat 2 tablespoons of the olive oil in a pan and add the finely chopped garlic. When it begins to colour, add the tomatoes with their juices, and squash them. Add some salt and pepper, and cook briskly for 15 minutes.

2 Meanwhile heat the rest of the oil in a separate pan, and add the mushrooms. Lightly salt, and let them cook gently for 5 minutes. Add the chopped parsley and keep warm.

3 Cook the pasta in rolling, boiling, salted water until *al dente*. Drain and turn into a heated serving dish. Add the tomato sauce, stirring thoroughly, and then the mushrooms. Stir well and serve at once.

Mushrooms contain a little protein, almost no fat, and are a good source of riboflavin, Vitamin B2. This is important for brain function, and is linked to the proper absorption of iron.

PASTA E PISELLI

Pasta and Peas

Italians love the pea season in June, and in order to enjoy tender young peas they have developed many, many pea recipes, one of the most famous being *Risi e Bisi* (*see* page 73). This recipe here is one of my pasta and pea favourites, a great dish for a family as peas seem to be so popular with children.

SERVES 4

4 tablespoons best-quality
   olive oil
1 onion
2 garlic cloves, peeled
750g peas in the pod, shelled
275g (10 oz) spaghetti

sea salt and freshly ground
   black pepper
a handful of fresh mint,
   finely chopped
freshly grated Parmesan
   to taste (optional)

1 In a medium saucepan gently fry the onion in the olive oil. When the onion is softened, add the garlic and gently coat in oil.

2 Now add all the peas, and mix well to coat them with oil, onion and garlic. Add 3 tablespoons water, place the lid on the pan, and very gently cook for 7 minutes.

3 Meanwhile cook the pasta in rolling, boiling, salted water until *al dente*, then drain.

4 Toss the sauce into the pasta with plenty of seasoning, the mint and some grated Parmesan to taste. Serve at once.

Peas, being the seeds of the plant, are extremely rich in nutrients, among them Vitamins A, B, C and E, and many minerals. They contain soluble fibre, can help control blood sugar, and may help to lower blood pressure. In folk medicine, the pea's primary claim to fame is as an anti-fertility agent, and this has been echoed by several conventional medical studies.

TAGLIATELLE AGLI ASPARAGI
Tagliatelle with Asparagus

There are many varieties of asparagus, so do experiment with this particular sauce. All varieties will work well, but I especially like sprue, the very thin green stalks which are tender and sweet, known as *selvatica* or 'wild' asparagus in Italy. Using green and yellow tagliatelle together – what the Italians call *paglia e fieno*, 'straw and hay' – makes the dish look very pretty.

SERVES 4

450g (1 lb) asparagus
sea salt and freshly ground
black pepper
100g (3½ oz) unsalted butter
1 slice stale white bread,
made into large crumbs
200 ml (7 fl oz) double cream
275g (10 oz) mixed green
and yellow tagliatelle
(ribbon noodles)

50g (2 oz) Fontina cheese,
grated
a handful of fresh basil, torn
a handful of fresh flat-leaf
parsley, finely chopped
freshly grated Parmesan
to taste (optional)

1 Wash the asparagus, and remove any tough base stalks. Place in a large shallow pan with a lid, add some sea salt, and cover with boiling water. Cook for about 8 minutes: this will depend on the size of the asparagus, so do use your judgement. Drain and plunge into cold water to stop the cooking. Drain again, and cut into 2 cm (¾ in) lengths, discarding any tough parts.

2 Melt the butter in a large pan, add the breadcrumbs, and cook gently, stirring all the time, for about 2 minutes. Now add the cream. Stir well, then add the asparagus and some black pepper to taste. Cook for 5 minutes, then keep warm.

3 Cook the pasta in plenty of rolling, boiling, salted water until *al dente*. Drain and add the asparagus sauce. Add the grated Fontina cheese, the basil and parsley, and mix well.

4 Check and adjust the seasoning, and serve at once, with Parmesan to taste if desired.

Asparagus is a natural blood cleanser due to its Vitamin A content. The Vitamin B it contains is good for nervous disorders. May and June are the natural season for the vegetable, so make sure you enjoy this dish often at that time!

PAPPARDELLE DELLE COLLINE DI FIRENZE

Pappardelle from the Hills of Florence

Ewe's milk Ricotta cheese may be hard to find, but good delis should stock it or will be able to get it for you. Ordinary Ricotta, made from pasteurised cow's milk, will happily substitute. We make our own Ricotta at the school, from goat's milk.

SERVES 4

2 tablespoons olive oil
1 onion, peeled and chopped
1 carrot, peeled and chopped
1 celery stick, chopped
1 garlic clove, peeled and crushed
200 g (7 oz) tomato passata
150 ml (¼ pint) white wine

sea salt and freshly ground black pepper
275 g (10 oz) pappardelle (wide ribbon noodles)
1 x 200 g (7 oz) tub fresh ewe's milk Ricotta cheese
a handful of fresh basil, torn
freshly grated Parmesan to taste

1 Heat the oil in a medium saucepan and add the chopped vegetables; stir well and cook gently until they change colour.

2 Add the garlic, tomato passata, wine, salt and pepper, lower the heat and simmer for 25 minutes, covered. Stir occasionally.

3 Meanwhile, boil the pasta in plenty of rolling, boiling, salted water until *al dente*, then drain.

4 Crumble the Ricotta into a tureen, pour over the hot pasta, sauce and basil, and mix well. Serve with plenty of Parmesan to taste, and garnish with more basil if liked.

As it is a whey cheese, Ricotta is very light and highly digestible – good for those who have stomach problems or who are unwell. I call Ricotta a 'store-cupboard ingredient', as I can find so many uses for it. Passata is tomato which has been chopped and sieved, leaving behind the seeds. It can be bought in jars and in cartons.

TAGLIATELLE CON CIPOLLE

Tagliatelle with Onion Sauce

Experiment with the many different types of onion available. Red onions from Tropea, in Calabria, are delicious because the soil is so good. You could use white onions instead, which have a very good flavour, or a combination of the two. Simple, satisfying and surprisingly good.

SERVES 4

100 g (3½ oz) unsalted butter
450 g (1 lb) onions, peeled
    and thinly sliced
150 ml (¼ pint) double cream
sea salt and freshly ground
    black pepper
a large pinch of freshly
    grated nutmeg

a handful of fresh flat-leaf
    parsley, finely chopped
275 g (10 oz) tagliatelle
    (ribbon noodles)
freshly grated Parmesan
    to taste

1 Melt the butter and cook the onion in a covered pan over a low heat until soft. Do not let the onion turn brown. Cover with a little water, approximately 4 tablespoons, and cook with the lid on, simmering for 20 minutes.

2 Purée the cooked onion, then add the cream, salt, pepper, nutmeg and parsley. Keep warm.

3 Cook the pasta in rolling, boiling, salted water until *al dente*, then drain and toss into the sauce. Mix very well, and serve with freshly grated Parmesan to taste.

Onions have antiseptic properties, and are digestive; the cream and cheese both add protein to the dish.

SPAGHETTI ALLA NAPOLETANA
Spaghetti with Tomato and Basil Sauce

There are many different recipes for tomato sauce – including several in this chapter – but this is my grandmother's basic one. Naples is famous for its tomatoes, particularly the San Marzano, which is known as the 'true' Italian plum tomato. It is different from the others in shape and flavour: it has 'shoulders', and a drier but sweeter flesh. This is also the tomato most commonly dried in the hot southern sun.

SERVES 4

3 tablespoons best-quality
   olive oil
1 onion, peeled and chopped
750 g (1 lb 12 oz) ripe tomatoes,
   roughly chopped
sea salt and freshly ground
   black pepper

275 g (10 oz) spaghetti
a handful of fresh basil, torn
25 g (1 oz) unsalted butter,
   cut into pieces
freshly grated Parmesan
   to taste

1 Heat the oil in a heavy pan, add the onion and fry gently for 5 minutes. Add the tomatoes, and some salt and pepper. Cook gently, covered, for 20 minutes.

2 Meanwhile, cook the spaghetti in plenty of rolling, boiling, salted water until *al dente*, then drain thoroughly.

3 Mix the pasta and tomato sauce together. Add the torn basil and the butter, and toss well. Serve at once with freshly grated Parmesan to taste.

Basil seeds are readily available to buy in Italy, particularly in the markets. There are two types: the lattugha *and the Genovese. The latter is for making pesto and has smaller, more flavourful leaves; the former has larger, slightly coarse leaves, which are for tearing and adding to a dish at the last minute.*

SPAGHETTI CON POMODORI E RUCOLA

Spaghetti with Fresh Tomatoes and Rocket

Try to buy wild rocket which has large, pungent leaves. You should find large bundles in good delis and in markets. Supermarkets sell tiny bags of French rocket which I think is not so flavourful (and the bags are very expensive).

SERVES 4

275 g (10 oz) red, ripe plum
    tomatoes
2 garlic cloves, peeled and
    finely chopped
100 g (3½ oz) rocket, coarsely
    chopped
grated zest of 1 unwaxed lemon

1½ tablespoons good-quality
    olive oil
sea salt and freshly ground
    black pepper
275 g (10 oz) spaghetti
freshly grated Parmesan
    to taste (optional)

1 Skin the tomatoes. Plunge them into boiling water for 20 seconds, then plunge into very cold water. Slip off the skins, and finely chop the flesh.

2 Place the tomato dice in a large bowl together with the garlic, rocket, lemon zest, olive oil, salt and pepper. Leave for a minimum of 30 minutes.

3 Cook the pasta in plenty of rolling, boiling, salted water until *al dente*, then drain well.

4 Stir the sauce into the pasta. Serve at once, with Parmesan to taste if desired.

A couple of tomato plants in a grow-bag, sturdy window-box or even a pot, can yield an amazing number of fruit in late summer. When freshly plucked they are bursting with flavour and nutrients, particularly Vitamins A and C.

PASTA AL CARTOCCIO

Spaghetti Baked in Parchment Paper

This is a dish for maximum visual effect. It is perfect for a dinner party, as the flavours and aromas are trapped inside the parchment paper, released only when the paper is slashed open. It's also good for a picnic or lunch in the garden; pasta cools down very quickly after being drained and tossed in its sauce, but wrapped in its paper packaging, it remains wonderfully hot. And parcels always produce a great element of surprise!

SERVES 4

2 tablespoons olive oil
1 large garlic clove, peeled
   but left whole
450g (1 lb) ripe fresh
   tomatoes, chopped
sea salt and freshly ground
   black pepper
1 teaspoon fresh hot red chilli

pepper (*peperoncino*),
   de-seeded and chopped
275g (10 oz) spaghetti
10 black olives, pitted
a handful of fresh flat-leaf
   parsley, chopped
freshly grated Parmesan
   to taste

1 Pre-heat the oven to 200°C / 400°F/gas mark 6. Prepare four pieces of parchment paper, each about 30 x 20 cm (12 x 8 in).

2 Heat the oil in a saucepan over a medium heat, and when warm, add the garlic and sauté for 2 minutes.

3 Discard the garlic, add the chopped tomato to the flavoured oil in the pan, and simmer for 20 minutes, stirring occasionally with a wooden spoon. Season with salt and pepper and add the chilli. Pass the contents of the pan through a food mill or liquidiser. Return to the pan and reduce over a medium heat for 10 minutes.

4 Meanwhile cook the pasta in rolling, boiling, salted water for half the time indicated on the packet only, then drain well.

5 Add the olives and half the parsley to the tomato sauce, and mix in the pasta. Adjust the seasoning. Place the portions of pasta in the middle of each piece of parchment paper, and scrunch the edges of each package to tightly close it. Place the packages in a roasting tin and bake for approximately 7 minutes, depending on the thickness of the spaghetti you have chosen.

6 Remove the tin from the oven, and place each package on a warm plate. Guests open their own packages, and sprinkle the insides with the remaining parsley leaves and some Parmesan to taste.

I always use flat-leaf parsley because it is easier to clean and chop, and because it just tastes better than curly. Parsley is full of iron, and is a stimulant for the liver, something the Italians are obsessed with and talk about on a daily basis!

SPAGHETTI ALLA NORCINA
Spaghetti with Truffles or Mushrooms

Truffles are synonymous with Italy. The white Alba truffle is the principal prize in Piedmont. To sniff them out, dogs are specially trained from puppies using cheese scented with truffles. Black truffles from Norcia, in Umbria, are not so prized, but in my opinion have more flavour. Winter truffles, *d'inverno*, have more flavour than those of the summer, *l'estate*.

SERVES 3–4

2 tablespoons olive oil

1 black truffle, sliced, or
  55 g (2 oz) dried *porcini*,
  reconstituted (*see* below)

1 garlic clove, peeled and
  crushed

a handful of fresh flat-leaf
  parsley, chopped

sea salt and freshly ground
  black pepper

275 g (10 oz) spaghetti

a handful of fresh basil, torn

freshly grated Parmesan
  to taste

1 Heat the oil in a heavy pan, add the truffle or drained porcini, and cook gently for 5 minutes. Remove from the heat and add the garlic and parsley. Return to the heat and cook gently for a few more minutes. Season to taste with salt and pepper.

2 Cook the spaghetti in plenty of rolling, boiling, salted water until *al dente*. Drain thoroughly then pile into a warmed serving dish.

3 Pour the sauce over the spaghetti, mix well, then add the finely torn basil leaves. Serve with plenty of Parmesan to taste.

To reconstitute dried porcini, *always use cold water so as not to draw out too much flavour from the mushrooms themselves. Use a minumum quantity of water for the same reason. Cover the mushrooms with water in a bowl and leave for 10 minutes. Pick them out of the water rather than strain them through a sieve (thus leaving any grit in the bowl). You could use the strained soaking water as stock.*

SPAGHETTI VESUVIO

Spaghetti with Vesuvius Sauce

The volcano Vesuvius is near Naples which is where I first ate this dish. In fact, I was eating it and looking at the gently steaming volcano at the same time!

SERVES 3–4

1 tablespoon olive oil

1 x 400g (14 oz) can Italian plum tomatoes

1 garlic clove, peeled and crushed

1 teaspoon dried oregano

sea salt and freshly ground black pepper

275g (10 oz) spaghetti

200g (7 oz) Mozzarella cheese, diced

55g (2 oz) freshly grated Parmesan

1 Warm the oil very gently in a pan, and add the tomatoes with their juices and the garlic. Stir in the oregano, salt and pepper, and cook rapidly for 20 minutes.

2 While the sauce is cooking, cook the pasta in rolling, boiling, salted water until *al dente*, then drain well.

3 Add the tomato sauce and the diced Mozzarella to the pasta. Toss rapidly, then cover and leave for about 2 minutes so that the Mozzarella begins to melt and look like streams of molten lava.

4 Serve at once, with the Parmesan sprinkled on top.

Italians preserve their own fresh tomatoes when there is a glut. When they run out, though, they always seem to go for cans of tomatoes, rather than cartons. These are better value for money and have a much better flavour. We should never be too disparaging about canned tomatoes: canning is an ancient, but entirely reliable, method of preserving, and the tomatoes used are of the best possible quality and freshness.

TORTELLI DI PATATE

Potato Tortelli

This recipe is dedicated to my father, a great potato lover and grower. You might find the combination of pasta and potato strange, but I promise you that you'll be pleased with the result. Despite consisting of two types of carbohydrate, the tortelli are surprisingly light.

SERVES 6

Pasta

250 g (9 oz) Italian 00 plain flour

250 g (9 oz) fine semolina

2 teaspoons sea salt

5 free-range eggs

1 tablespoon olive oil

Filling

600 g (1 lb 5 oz) potatoes, scrubbed

100 g (3½ oz) freshly grated Parmesan

2 garlic cloves, peeled and chopped

a handful of fresh flat-leaf parsley, chopped

4 ripe tomatoes, skinned and diced

½ teaspoon freshly grated nutmeg

1 free-range egg, lightly beaten

sea salt and freshly ground black pepper

To serve

freshly grated Parmesan

1 To make the pasta, heap the flour and semolina into a mound on the work surface. Sprinkle over the salt and mix well. Hollow out a well in the centre into which you break the eggs. Add the olive oil and, with much care and patience, gradually work the eggs and oil into the flour until you have a slab of dough. Shape this into a ball and leave under a tea towel to rest while you prepare the filling.

2 Boil the potatoes in their skins until tender, then drain, peel and mash. Mix in the remaining ingredients, apart from the egg, adding salt and pepper to taste. Last of all, mix in the egg.

3 Roll out the pasta dough wafer thin and cut into strips 3 cm (1¼ in) wide. Over half of these strips spoon 5–6 tablespoons of stuffing at well-spaced intervals. Cover each strip with another strip of pasta. Seal by pressing down well on the borders. Cut each strip into 3 cm (1¼ in) tortelli that you place on a lightly floured tea towel as you go. (The action of cutting seals the pasta sides together.)

4 Boil the tortelli in plenty of rolling, boiling, salted water. Drain when cooked but still firm to the bite. Make sure that the pasta is well cooked in the thickest part.

5 Serve the tortelli with Parmesan cheese.

Over years of experience this pasta-dough recipe has proved to be the most successful of all, the semolina adding colour, flavour and texture. You can use the dough to make pappardelle, tagliatelle, tortellini, ravioli, lasagne etc. Cooking the potatoes in their skins means that the potato flesh will absorb much less water than if they were peeled. It also means that the starch remains in the flesh, rather than leaching into the water, which allows the potato to retain more flavour. Leave the potatoes until cool enough to handle, then simply slide the skins off.

SPAGHETTI ALLE OLIVE

Spaghetti with Olives

There is such a wide variety of olives available now, that you can use your imagination and experiment with the type that you like the most. Choose green, violet or black, and drain them well before using to get rid of as much brine as possible. You can marinate your own. The Gaeta olive, which comes from near Rome, is wonderful rinsed, dried then left for ten days in an infusion of extra-virgin olive oil with fennel seeds, garlic and a little chilli.

SERVES 4

150 ml (¼ pint) good-quality olive oil

1 yellow pepper, cored, de-seeded and sliced

3 tomatoes, skinned and chopped

sea salt and freshly ground black pepper

100 g (3½ oz) black olives, halved and pitted

275 g (10 oz) spaghetti

65 g (2½ oz) Pecorino or freshly grated Parmesan cheese

a handful of fresh flat-leaf parsley, finely chopped

1 Heat the oil in a heavy pan, and add the sliced yellow pepper, tomato and salt and pepper to taste. Cover and simmer gently for 20 minutes, stirring occasionally. Add the olives and cook for 5 minutes.

2 Meanwhile cook the spaghetti in plenty of rolling, boiling, salted water until *al dente*. Drain thoroughly and add to the sauce.

3 Fold gently to mix, then pile into a warmed serving dish and sprinkle with the cheese and parsley. Serve at once.

Olives contain good quantities of Vitamins A and E (although less of the latter than the oil). Like the oil, they contain monounsaturated fatty acids, so are protective of the heart and blood vessels, and can help lower cholesterol levels. Olives that have been kept in brine contain a high level of sodium.

SPAGHETTI AGLIO OLIO E PEPERONCINO
Spaghetti with Garlic and Chilli Oil

This is definitely a standby recipe, but it is simple and tasty. I often cook it when I've just come back from holiday and there's nothing else in the fridge.

SERVES 4

275 g (10 oz) spaghetti
sea salt and freshly ground
    black pepper
4 tablespoons best-quality
    olive oil
2 garlic cloves, peeled

1 fresh hot red chilli pepper
    (*peperoncino*), seeded and
    chopped
a handful of fresh flat-leaf
    parsley, finely chopped
freshly grated Parmesan
    to taste (optional)

1 Cook the spaghetti in plenty of rolling, boiling, salted water until *al dente*.

2 Meanwhile, heat the oil in a heavy pan, add the garlic and chilli, and fry gently until the garlic has coloured slightly.

3 Drain the spaghetti thoroughly and pile into a warmed serving dish.

4 Discard the garlic and chilli. Add the parsley to the flavoured oil, then mix well and pour over the spaghetti. Serve at once, with Parmesan to taste if liked.

Garlic has many incredible health-giving properties: it contains vitamins and many minerals, and sulphur compounds which are responsible for its flavour and odour. The smell of it cooking stimulates the gastric juices, so before you've even eaten it, it's started the process of good digestion.

LASAGNE CON MELANZANE

Lasagne with Aubergines

Lasagne has been enjoyed in Italy since Roman times. Baking pasta in layers with vegetables is healthy, tasty and very filling, and this is a perfect dish for sharing with family or friends.

SERVES 4

4 tablespoons good-quality
   olive oil
1 large garlic clove, peeled
   and crushed
1 large white onion, peeled
   and chopped
1 x 400 g (14 oz) can chopped
   tomatoes
3 tablespoons red wine

sea salt and freshly ground
   black pepper
1 firm, ripe, large aubergine
175 g (6 oz) egg lasagne
   (shop-bought pasta sheets,
   no pre-cooking required)
450 g (1 lb) Mozzarella cheese,
   sliced
a handful of fresh basil leaves

1 In a large saucepan heat half the olive oil, then add the garlic and cook gently for a few minutes. Add the onion and sauté until soft. Lower the heat, add the tomatoes, wine, salt and pepper, and simmer for 20 minutes. Set aside.

2 Cut the aubergine into lengthways slices 3 mm (⅛ in) thick, and place in layers in a colander. Sprinkle salt between the layers and leave for 15 minutes. Rinse to remove the salt, and pat dry.

3 Meanwhile, pre-heat the oven to 200°C/400°F/gas mark 6.

4 In a frying pan, heat some of the remaining oil, just enough to cover the bottom. Sauté the aubergine slices quickly, about 2 minutes on each side, or until soft. Drain on kitchen paper. Continue in this fashion, using more oil as needed.

5 To assemble the lasagne, spread one-third of the tomato sauce over the base of a lasagne dish (about 25 cm/10 in square). Add a layer of lasagne sheets and then a little more sauce, then half the aubergine and Mozzarella slices. Season the cheese and sprinkle with some basil leaves. Continue in this way, finishing off with a layer of tomato sauce. Cover with foil.

6 Bake the lasagne in the pre-heated oven for 25 minutes until bubbling.

This baked dish can be made a day ahead of time, so is particularly useful when entertaining. In Italy, aubergines are known as 'poor man's meat' because they are so substantial and satisfying.

LASAGNE DI RADICCHIO ALLA TREVISANA

Radicchio Lasagne

I have a tremendous love for radicchio, having watched it being grown by my father. From planting to harvest is six weeks, so it would be a good vegetable to grow at home. There are two varieties: the round, which is the most common, and the Treviso, which is long and thin. Do try to get the Treviso – order it from your greengrocer – as it is very much less bitter and much more flavourful.

SERVES 4

3 heads Treviso radicchio

3 tablespoons olive oil

1 medium fennel bulb, peeled and
   quartered

300g (11 oz) dried lasagne verdi
   (green pasta sheets)

1 onion, peeled and finely chopped

85g (3 oz) butter

55g (2 oz) plain white flour

1 garlic clove, peeled and crushed

500 ml (17 fl oz) milk

sea salt and freshly ground black pepper

150g (5½ oz) Dolcelatte cheese,
   cut into cubes

1 Pre-heat the oven to 200°C/400°F/gas mark 6.

2 Quarter the radicchio, wash well and pat dry. Place on a baking tray and drizzle the olive oil over. Bake in the pre-heated oven (or put under a pre-heated grill) for 10 minutes. The radicchio pieces will change colour and become slightly charred; this is correct, as the flavour will be at its best. Set aside.

3 Meanwhile, steam the fennel pieces over boiling water, about 12 minutes (it should be slightly *al dente*). Remove and finely chop.

4 Cook the lasagne in plenty of rolling, boiling, salted water until *al dente*. Drain and set aside.

5 Now for the sauce. Cook the onion in a saucepan in the butter until it is softened and golden. Add the flour, garlic and steamed fennel and cook for a few minutes to remove the raw taste from the flour. Now add the milk, and some salt and pepper. Remove from the heat and stir vigorously with a wooden spoon.

6 Place back on the heat and bring to the boil, stirring continuously until thickened. Add the cubed Dolcelatte and stir well. Check the seasoning.

7 To assemble the dish, place a layer of sauce in an oval ovenproof dish followed by a layer of radicchio and a layer of pasta, and continue in this fashion until all the sauce, radicchio and lasagne have been used up. Finish with sauce on top.

8 Place in the pre-heated oven (still at the same temperature as above), and bake for 20 minutes until golden.

An elderly lady friend told me that soaking radicchio for half an hour removes much of its bitterness. However, it is this very bitterness that the Italians crave, believing that it is a stimulant of the liver, the organ which is the cornerstone of health.

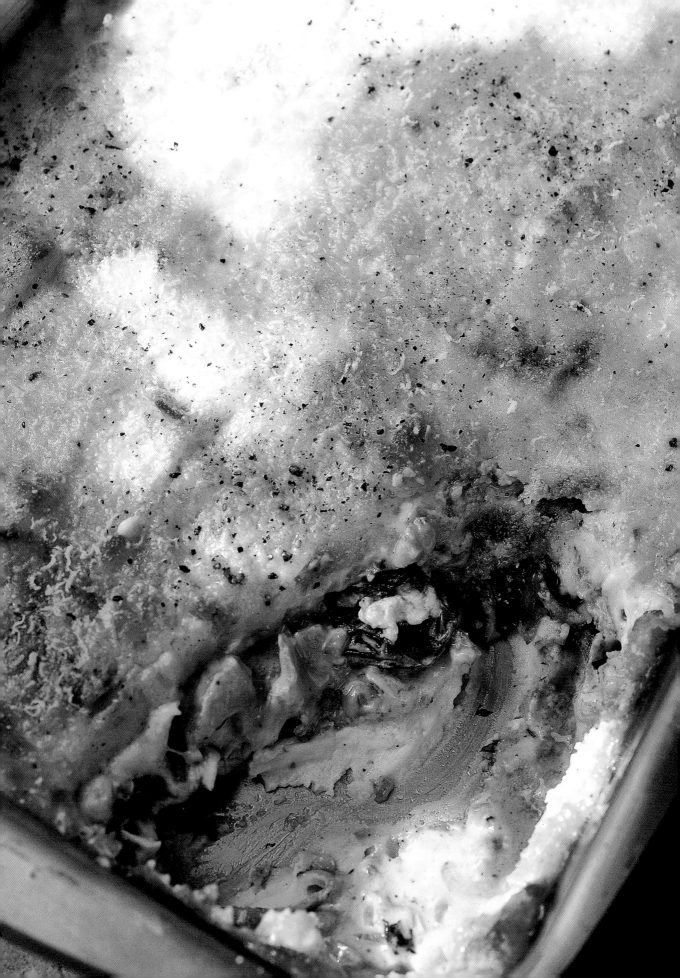

FARFALLE ALLA POLCERVERASCA

Pasta with Butter and Marjoram

This is a recipe I'd like to dedicate to tired cooks. If you've been working all day you want something tasty and simple, and the flavours here just seem to hit the right note. It's also very quick, just what you need when you're hungry. (If you want it to cook even more quickly, use a thinner pasta.)

SERVES 4

85 g (3 oz) unsalted butter
1 tablespoon pine kernels, chopped
1 tablespoon chopped fresh marjoram
sea salt and freshly ground black pepper
275 g (10 oz) farfalle (bows)
85 g (3 oz) freshly grated Parmesan

1 Melt the butter in a small pan, add the pine kernels and marjoram, and heat, stirring, for 1 minute. Season well.

2 Meanwhile, cook the farfalle in rolling, boiling, salted water until *al dente*. Drain and mix well with marjoram and butter sauce.

3 Sprinkle with Parmesan, and serve at once.

Marjoram is good for migraine, and for insomnia, so try to include it in a dish you eat at night. It is also a good antiseptic herb, guarding against infection, but not as strong as its sister, oregano.

VERMICELLI AL RANCETTO

Vermicelli in Tomato and Marjoram Sauce

This sauce is incredibly simple. If you grow your own herbs, it's wonderful to infuse some freshly picked marjoram in the tomato sauce, to give a pungent flavour. You could replace the marjoram with another herb, such as oregano or a soft-leaved thyme.

SERVES 3–4

4 tablespoons good-quality olive oil
1 onion, peeled and sliced
1 tablespoon chopped fresh marjoram
a handful of fresh flat-leaf parsley,
    finely chopped
just over ½ x 400 g (14 oz) can Italian
    plum tomatoes
sea salt and freshly ground black pepper
275 g (10 oz) vermicelli (thin spaghetti)
55 g (2 oz) Pecorino cheese, grated

1 Heat the oil in a medium saucepan. Add the onion and sauté until golden. Add the marjoram, parsley and tomatoes, and break the latter up with a wooden spoon. Season with salt and pepper, and simmer, covered, for 20 minutes.

2 Cook the vermicelli in boiling, salted water until *al dente*, then drain thoroughly.

3 Add the sauce and cheese to the hot pasta, mix well, and serve at once.

Marjoram is also known as a digestive herb, and its inclusion in a dish helps your body to assimilate the other constituents of the dish.

44

PENNE AL CAVOLFIORE
Penne with Cauliflower

This vegetable is most commonly found covered with a cheese sauce. Please think again, and use it with pasta as here, married with chilli, which is a fantastic combination. Cauliflowers are particularly associated with southern Italy, so don't expect them too often on menus in the north.

SERVES 4

1½ tablespoons olive oil

2 garlic cloves, peeled and chopped

1 small, fresh, hot red chilli pepper (*peperoncino*), whole or chopped

1 small cauliflower, cut into florets

½ x 400 g (14 oz) can chopped tomatoes

250 ml (9 fl oz) home-made vegetable stock (*see* page 61) or water

275 g (10 oz) penne (quills)

200 ml (7 fl oz) double cream

a handful of fresh flat-leaf parsley, chopped

4 fresh sage leaves, finely chopped

sea salt and freshly ground black pepper

1 Heat the oil and add the chopped garlic and the whole or chopped chilli pepper. Cook for 3 minutes on a low flame, then add the cauliflower florets. After 5 minutes add the chopped tomatoes in their juices, the herbs and seasoning, and cook gently for 10 minutes.

2 Add the stock; depending on the amount of cauliflower, you may need less stock, so do use your judgement.

3 Leave to simmer while you cook the pasta in plenty of rolling, boiling, salted water until *al dente*.

4 Add the cream to the cauliflower mixture. Remove the chilli if whole, then squash the cauliflower roughly with a potato masher.

5 Drain the pasta and stir in the herbs and sauce. Serve at once.

Cauliflower contains Vitamins A, B and C, and the minerals potassium, iron and calcium. It's said to be good for arthritic and rheumatic conditions.

PENNETTE IN PADELLA

Penne in the Pan

Penne are tubes of pasta that resemble small quill pens. They are either ridged or smooth, and can vary in length (pennette are slightly smaller than penne). This recipe was devised by the Lungarotti family who own a charming hotel, vineyard and wine museum in Torgiano, Umbria, very near where I teach. They produce some excellent wine, their most famous one being San Giorgio. If you get an opportunity to taste this wine, you will not be disappointed.

SERVES 4

- 1 medium, firm and ripe aubergine
- sea salt and freshly ground black pepper
- 4 tablespoons best-quality olive oil
- 3 tablespoons red wine
- 1 small onion, peeled and finely chopped
- 1 garlic clove, peeled and crushed
- 1 x 400g (14 oz) can chopped tomatoes
- 275g (10 oz) pennette or penne (quills)
- 2 tablespoons double cream
- 1 tablespoon finely chopped fresh oregano
- 1 tablespoon finely chopped fresh flat-leaf parsley
- 2 tablespoons freshly grated Parmesan

1 Cut the aubergine into small cubes, sprinkle with salt, place in a bowl, cover and weight down. Leave for 15 minutes. Rinse the aubergine cubes well to remove the salt, and pat dry.

2 Heat the oil in a frying pan, add the aubergine and fry for 5 minutes until golden. Add the wine and simmer for 5 minutes, then season with salt and pepper.

3 Add the onion, garlic and tomatoes to the aubergine, bring up to the boil and simmer for 15 minutes (add a little water if necessary).

4 Cook the pasta in rolling, boiling, salted water until *al dente*.

5 Just before serving the sauce, stir the cream, oregano and parsley into the sauce, and check the seasoning.

6 Drain the pasta, toss with the sauce and heat through. Serve hot with the Parmesan sprinkled on top.

Many people believe that it isn't necessary these days to salt or 'degorge' aubergines, but I think it's still vital. The aubergines are tenderer, have more flavour and do not absorb so much of the cooking oil.

RIGATONI CON BROCCOLETTI E GORGONZOLA

Pasta with Broccoli and Gorgonzola

The combination of the four main ingredients here is particularly tasty, satisfying and nutritionally rich. Do try to find Italian pine kernels (from *Pinus pinea*, the stone pine), as they are longer, thinner, and creamier – and therefore tastier – than the Asian varieties. They are incredibly expensive, even in Italy, as acid rain in Europe has diminished the yield. Keep them in the fridge once the packet is opened to prevent the oils from turning rancid.

SERVES 4

40g (1½ oz) pine kernels

100g (3½ oz) broccoli florets

100g (3½ oz) cauliflower florets

1 red onion, peeled and finely chopped

2 tablespoons olive oil

1 teaspoon chopped fresh thyme

sea salt and freshly ground black pepper

275g (10 oz) rigatoni (short, ribbed noodles)

100g (3½ oz) Gorgonzola cheese, diced

1 Toast the pine kernels on a sheet of foil under the grill, turning them frequently until they are golden.

2 Steam the broccoli and cauliflower for about 8 minutes, depending on size, or until just tender.

3 Meanwhile, cook the onion in the oil until softened, then add the thyme and some salt and pepper.

4 Cook the pasta in plenty of rolling, boiling, salted water until *al dente*. Drain well.

5 Add the cheese to the onion along with the pine kernels, broccoli and cauliflower. Toss thoroughly into the pasta. Adjust the seasonings and serve.

All blue cheeses contain natural penicillin, which helps to boost the immune system. This particular sauce is very good for you (and tastes delicious).

BUCATINI ALLA SIRACUSANA
Syracusan-style Pasta

There is no pasta dish to my mind that has more zing and personality than this one, from Syracuse in Sicily. It has all the right attributes of spiciness, flavour, colour and drama, all very characteristic of Sicilian food and life, both in turn displaying many influences from North Africa and Greece.

SERVES 4

1 small aubergine
sea salt and freshly ground
   black pepper
2 tablespoons olive oil
2 garlic cloves, peeled and
   crushed
3 ripe plum tomatoes, chopped
1 small yellow pepper,
   de-seeded and cut into
   thin strips

10 black olives, pitted and
   chopped
10 capers, rinsed and drained
275 g (10 oz) bucatini
   (thick, hollow spaghetti),
   or any favourite pasta shape
a handful of fresh basil,
   roughly torn
freshly grated Pecorino
   Romano cheese, to taste

1 Cut the aubergine into cubes, then put in a colander, scatter with salt, weight down, cover and leave to degorge for 15 minutes. Rinse and pat dry.

2 In a large saucepan heat the olive oil and gently sauté the garlic until soft. Add the aubergine and cook until the cubes become soft and golden: about 8 minutes.

3 Add the tomatoes, pepper, olives, capers and seasoning. Mix well, cover the pan and cook for 20 minutes.

4 Cook the pasta in plenty of rolling, boiling, salted water until *al dente*. Drain and return to the pan. Add the sauce and basil, and mix well. Pass the cheese around to be sprinkled on top.

Never add fresh basil at the beginning of cooking, always at the end, because it is so tender, and its volatile oils are destroyed by heat. These oils can also be lost on the chopping board, which is why I always tear or shred it.

ROTOLO RIPIENO

Spinach Pasta Roll

I've only eaten this pasta roll in the north of Italy. I'm using a classic spinach filling here, but you could also try a mushroom or Ricotta filling. It makes an impressive dinner-party piece, particularly memorable because the grilling at the end makes the pasta become crisp.

SERVES 4–6

Pasta

**150g (5 oz) Italian 00
   plain flour**
150g (5 oz) fine semolina
a pinch of sea salt
2 large free-range eggs
1 tablespoon olive oil

Filling

4 tomatoes
350g (12 oz) fresh spinach
175g (6 oz) Ricotta cheese
freshly grated nutmeg
**sea salt and freshly ground
   black pepper**

To Serve

25g (1 oz) butter
**25g (1 oz) freshly grated
   Parmesan**

1 Make the pasta as for Potato Tortelli, using the smaller quantity of ingredients here (*see* pages 34–5). Cover and set aside.

2 Put the tomatoes in a bowl, cover with boiling water for about 30 seconds, then plunge into cold water, drain and skin. Chop the flesh.

3 Wash the spinach and put in a saucepan with only the water still clinging to the leaves. Cook for 5 minutes then drain well, squeezing out the excess water.

4 Finely chop the spinach and put in a bowl. Add the tomato, Ricotta, nutmeg, salt and pepper and mix well together.

4 Roll out the pasta dough to a rectangular sheet about 3 mm (⅛ in) thick. Spread the filling over the dough, leaving a 5 mm (¼ in) border. Roll up the dough like a Swiss roll, and then wrap in a piece of muslin, securing the ends with string.

5 Place the roll in a long, narrow, flameproof casserole or roasting tin, and cover with lightly salted cold water. Bring to the boil and simmer for 20 minutes. Remove the roll from the water and leave to cool for 5 minutes.

6 Remove the muslin and cut the roll into 2 cm (¾ in) thick slices. Place slightly overlapping in a buttered ovenproof dish. Melt the remaining butter and pour over the slices. Sprinkle with the Parmesan and grill for 7 minutes. Serve immediately.

Butter infused with sage leaves is excellent for drizzling over the top of the rotolo.

FETTUCCINE CON DUE FORMAGGI E PISTACCHI

Fettuccine with Two-cheese Sauce and Pistachios

This pasta dish is blissfully simple and very colourful because of the green nuts and leaves. It's a store-cupboard recipe, easy to put together at the end of the day. The fettuccine, being long and thin, is excellent with a rich cheese sauce.

SERVES 4

150 ml (¼ pint) double cream
40 g (1½ oz) Dolcelatte cheese
40 g (1½ oz) freshly grated
   Parmesan
25 g (1 oz) shelled pistachio nuts

sea salt and freshly ground
   black pepper
275 g (10 oz) fettuccine
   (ribbon noodles)
a handful of fresh basil, torn

1 Pour the cream into a saucepan and bring slowly to the boil. Reduce the heat, crumble in the Dolcelatte, and stir until melted and smooth. Add the Parmesan, and cook over a very low heat until thick and smooth, a few minutes only.

2 Roughly chop the pistachio nuts. Add to the sauce and season with salt and pepper to taste.

3 Cook the pasta in plenty of rolling, boiling, salted water until *al dente*. Drain, then stir in the sauce. Garnish with basil leaves and serve hot.

Pistachio nuts are related to the cashew nut and mango and, like all nuts, they are high in vegetable protein. This, allied with the cheese and pasta, makes for a dish rich in nutrients.

FETTUCCINE E CECI ALLA NAPOLETANA

Pasta with Chick Peas

This recipe is a good example of southern Italian cooking which does not rely heavily on meat, but provides carbohydrate and protein in the form of grain and pulses. The cheese provides extra nutrients.

SERVES 4

200 g (7 oz) dried chick peas
1 litre (1¾ pints) water
3 bay leaves
3 tablespoons best-quality olive oil
5 tomatoes, skinned and chopped
1 garlic clove, peeled and crushed

a handful of fresh flat-leaf parsley, chopped
sea salt and freshly ground black pepper
275 g (10 oz) fettuccine (ribbon noodles)
a handful of fresh basil, torn
freshly grated Parmesan to taste (optional)

1 Soak the chick peas overnight in plenty of cold water.

2 Drain and place in a large pan with the measured water and the bay leaves, bring to the boil and boil for 10 minutes, then turn the heat down and simmer for about 40 minutes or until tender.

3 Now add the oil, tomatoes, garlic and half the parsley to the chickpeas. Bring back to the boil, season, then add the fettuccine. Cook for 12 minutes approximately, or until the pasta is tender. Add more water if required.

4 Add the remaining parsley and the basil and serve immediately with Parmesan to taste if desired.

Vegetables and pulses do not contain all the essential amino acids and so are known as incomplete proteins – apart from soya beans, the only food of non-animal origin which is a complete protein. By combining grain and a pulse, as here, the nutritional value of the dish is considerably enhanced.

CANNELLONI CON VERDURE E FORMAGGIO

Cannelloni with Vegetables and Cheese

I have a great affinity with cannelloni, and in Italy we have many varieties. Many cannelloni dishes are made with pasta, but this one, traditional to Piacenza in Sicily, is constructed from *crespelle* or pancakes, and is particularly light. It can be made into a wonderful antipasto dish.

SERVES 4

Pancake batter

225 g (8 oz) plain flour

½ teaspoon sea salt

1½ teaspoons freshly grated nutmeg

2 large free-range eggs, beaten

1 large free-range egg yolk, beaten

350 ml (12 fl oz) whole milk

1 tablespoon unsalted butter, melted

3 tablespoons freshly grated Parmesan

freshly ground black pepper

Filling

350 g (12 oz) Ricotta cheese, well drained

1 large free-range egg

125 g (4½ oz) lightly cooked broccoli, chopped

3 tablespoons freshly grated Parmesan

4 ripe tomatoes, skinned, de-seeded and chopped

a handful of fresh flat-leaf parsley, chopped

1 teaspoon grated zest of unwaxed lemon

To cook and serve

3 tablespoons melted unsalted butter

freshly grated Parmesan to taste

1. Pre-heat the oven to 200° C/400°F/ gas mark 6.

2. To make the *crespella* (pancake) batter, sift the flour, salt and nutmeg together into a large bowl. Add the beaten eggs and egg yolk, the milk and melted butter. Whisk the mixture until smooth. If it seems too thin, add a little more flour; if it is too thick, add a little milk. Beat in the Parmesan and some pepper.

3. In a large bowl combine the Ricotta and the egg. Add the remaining filling ingredients and mix.

4. To cook the *crespelle*, lightly butter a 15–20 cm (6–8 in) crêpe pan or a frying pan, and heat over a medium heat. When hot, add a ladleful of the batter, and swirl the pan to make sure the pan is evenly coated with a thin layer of batter. Cook for 2 minutes or until lightly browned on the underside. Flip the *crespella* over and cook the other side until lightly browned.

5. Remove the *crespella* to a piece of kitchen paper and repeat the process. Lightly grease the pan every so often to prevent the batter from sticking. You should make about 8 pancakes.

6. Spread about an eighth of the filling over each *crespella* and roll up into a cylinder. Place them in a single layer, seam side down, in a suitably sized, buttered ovenproof dish. Drizzle the melted butter over them and sprinkle with Parmesan.

7. Bake for 10–15 minutes in the pre-heated oven until piping hot and golden. Then serve immediately.

RISOTTO

Pasta may rule in most of Italy but rice reigns in the north, and risotto is the preferred and most popular rice dish. You will find it everywhere from Milan to Venice and from Turin to Como, on restaurant menus and on family dining tables. It is a healthy dish, as the nutrients of the grain are usually melded with those of vegetables, and then grated Parmesan cheese is added, contributing its protein and calcium.

Risotto is a dish that is simple to prepare, nutritious, economical, versatile and – as you will discover – addictively delicious. It is prepared with a short-grain, highly glutinous rice grown in the Po Valley of northern Italy. This comes in several different varieties, the most important of which are *vialone nano*, *carnaroli* and *arborio*. *Vialone*, which has a slightly shorter grain, is used mostly in fishy risottos, *carnaroli* is normally allied with vegetables, and *arborio* can be used in most dishes. Risotto rice is special in that it absorbs to an unusual degree the flavours of the ingredients with which it's cooked. It also merges with its cooking liquid to create a consistency that the Italians call

all'onda ('with waves'), while each individual grain of rice remains firm and *al dente*. This combination of full-flavoured, still firm grains of rice, bound with the velvety base, is what gives risotto its unique quality and special character.

No matter what different *condimento* (flavouring or ingredient) is used, every risotto is created in basically the same way. A wide *sauté* pan with quite high sides should be used. The *riso* (rice) is first combined with a *soffritto* (a combination of fat and flavouring, usually butter and shallot) to coat it in fat. Simmering *brodo* (broth, which must be fresh and home-made) is then added gradually to the rice, allowing the rice to absorb one ladleful before adding the next. The rice is stirred continuously. When the grains are tender but still firm, there is usually a final addition of flavouring and seasoning (salt added at the beginning would toughen the rice). Then the rice is allowed to rest before being served on warm plates.

In Italy risotto, like pasta, is considered a *primo piatto*, the first course of a typical meal that might contain several courses brought to the table at carefully paced intervals.

BRODO DI VERDURE
Vegetable Stock

This is a basic vegetable stock, to be used in the making of all risottos, but can also be used as the base of a soup. Store it in the fridge for up to three days; it can also be frozen.

MAKES 1 LITRE (1¾ PINTS)

2 onions, peeled
12 whole cloves
1 garlic clove, peeled
6 carrots, scrubbed and trimmed
4 leeks, washed
2 celery sticks

40g (1½ oz) unsalted butter
1 tablespoon olive oil
4 bay leaves
2 sprigs fresh thyme
a handful of fresh flat-leaf parsley

1 Peel both onions, then stud one of them with the cloves. Chop the other onion, along with the garlic, carrots, leeks and celery.

2 Melt the butter and oil together in a large, heavy-based saucepan. Add the garlic and fry for 2 minutes. Add the chopped onion, carrot, leek, celery and the whole studded onion, and cook for 5–7 minutes until softened, stirring continuously.

3 Add 3 litres (5¼ pints) water, the bay leaves, thyme and parsley,

and bring to the boil. Cover, reduce the heat, and simmer for 1½ hours.

4 Remove from the heat and leave to cool for 1½ hours.

5 Return the pan to the heat and simmer for 15 minutes. Strain the stock through a sieve and return to the pan, discarding the vegetables. Boil rapidly until reduced by half.

6 Allow to cool completely before storing in the fridge.

I have not listed seasonings in the ingredients as everything depends on taste, and on the individual recipe in which you want to use the stock. And you must never add salt before the stock is reduced, as it would have the effect of concentrating the saltiness.

RISOTTO CON I FUNGHI

Wild Mushroom Risotto

This risotto is very popular in the mushroom season: September and October, and then January and February. You can use a variety of interesting mushrooms which we can find easily in specialist shops and supermarkets. Think of chestnut mushrooms, *girolles*, oyster mushrooms – and, of course, ceps or penny buns, the famous *porcini* of Italy.

SERVES 4

200g (7 oz) mixed wild
   mushrooms
2 garlic cloves, peeled and
   crushed
6 shallots, peeled and finely
   chopped
100g (4 oz) unsalted butter
sea salt and freshly ground
   black pepper
1 sprig fresh rosemary, finely
   chopped

350g (12 oz) *vialone nano*
   risotto rice
1 litre (1¾ pints) hot,
   home-made vegetable
   stock (*see* page 61)
125 ml (4½ fl oz) white wine,
   preferably dry
a handful of fresh flat-leaf
   parsley, chopped
85g (3 oz) freshly grated
   Parmesan

1 Wipe the mushrooms well to remove any grit, and then slice them.

2 Fry the garlic and shallot in half the butter until slightly coloured, then add the mushrooms, pepper and rosemary.

3 Add the rice and stir to coat in the mixture. Add a ladleful of hot stock and stir well until it has been absorbed by the rice. Keep adding the stock in this way, a ladleful at a time, until the stock is used up, stirring continuously. This takes about 18–20 minutes.

4 Add some salt, the wine, parsley, remaining butter and the Parmesan. Adjust the seasoning to taste.

5 Cover for 1 minute to allow the rice to rest. Serve on hot plates, with extra grated Parmesan if desired.

The secret of a good risotto is not to stop stirring, as this helps to develop the starch and make the risotto properly, authentically and deliciously creamy. Warm plates are important too, as otherwise the hot rice would adhere to the cold plate, ruining its consistency, which must remain 'wavy': all'onda.

RISOTTO ALLA MILANESE

Classic Saffron Risotto

Milan is the home of risotto, and although this particular risotto is very simple, it is probably the most enjoyed, most households making it at least once a week. The smell of saffron is haunting and the risotto is very comforting.

SERVES 4

150g (5½ oz) unsalted butter

1 tablespoon olive oil

6 shallots, peeled and finely chopped

sea salt and freshly ground black pepper

7 tablespoons dry white wine

1 litre (1¾ pints) hot, home-made Vegetable Stock (see page 61)

350g (12 oz) risotto rice (*vialone nano* is the best here)

¼ teaspoon powdered saffron

100g (3½ oz) freshly grated Parmesan

4 tablespoons single cream

a handful of fresh flat-leaf parsley, finely chopped

1 Melt the butter and oil in a medium saucepan, add the shallot and some pepper, and fry for 5 minutes until softened.

2 Add the wine and 7 tablespoons of the stock, and boil until reduced by half. Meanwhile keep the stock just below simmering point in a separate saucepan.

3 Add the rice to the shallot and reduced liquid, and cook for 5 minutes, stirring constantly on a medium heat. Add the saffron and the hot stock, a ladleful at a time, stirring well between each addition, until the rice is tender but firm, and the stock is used up. This should take about 18–20 minutes.

4 Remove from the heat and add some salt, the Parmesan, cream and parsley, and mix well.

5 Leave to stand for 1 minute to allow the rice to rest. Serve on hot plates, with extra grated Parmesan if desired.

Because saffron, the stamen of a crocus, is hand picked, it tends to be very expensive. There are many varieties, but here I use powdered because the colour is more even. Never be tempted to use more than a recipe states, as saffron is very strong. Spanish saffron is the best, but beware of imitations.

RISOTTO ALLA ZUCCA
Pumpkin Risotto

Pumpkin is eaten all year round in Italy, not just during the season. Fresh pumpkins are put in straw in cellars to preserve them; the flesh is bottled in olive oil and eaten as an antipasto. It is also used in pasta sauces, in tortelli, and in vegetable bakes.

SERVES 4

2 garlic cloves, peeled and crushed

25 g (1 oz) unsalted butter

2 teaspoons olive oil

6 shallots, peeled and finely chopped

500 g (18 oz) pumpkin, peeled, de-seeded and chopped

350 g (12 oz) *carnaroli* risotto rice

1 litre (1¾ pints) hot, home-made vegetable stock (*see* page 61)

sea salt and freshly ground black pepper

a handful of fresh flat-leaf parsley, chopped

4 tablespoons freshly grated Parmesan

1 Fry the garlic in the butter and oil until coloured. Add the shallot and pumpkin, and cook gently so that the latter softens.

2 Add the rice and stir to coat in the pumpkin mixture. Add ladlefuls of hot stock one at a time, stirring continuously, until it is all used up and the rice

is creamy. This should take about 18–20 minutes.

3 Stir in some salt and pepper, the parsley and Parmesan.

4 Cover for 1 minute to allow the rice to rest, then serve at once on warmed plates.

Pumpkin flesh contains many vitamins and minerals. The yellow flesh is packed with beta-carotene, the precursor of Vitamin A, so pumpkin is particularly good for the skin and the mucous membranes of the body. The seeds, which should always be saved for eating, are said to have a calming effect on the nervous system.

RISOTTO CON ZUCCHINI E FIORI

Risotto with Courgettes and their Flowers

This is a slightly indulgent recipe, as courgette flowers are not readily available unless you grow them yourself. I have seen them in shops – at a price – but they always look rather tired, although they can be revived in iced water. Give them a shake before use to dislodge any insects that might be lurking inside. Whenever I see *fiori di zucchini*, it means the onset of summer for me.

SERVES 4

5 tablespoons olive oil

8 young, tender and thin courgettes, sliced, whole flowers detached

6 shallots, peeled and sliced

350 g (12 oz) *carnaroli* risotto rice

sea salt and freshly ground black pepper

1 litre (1¾ pints) hot, home-made vegetable stock (*see* page 61)

a handful of fresh mint, finely chopped

a handful of fresh flat-leaf parsley, finely chopped

25 g (1 oz) unsalted butter

50 g (2 oz) freshly grated Parmesan

1 In a deep frying pan heat the oil, and fry the sliced courgettes for 2 minutes until tender.

2 Add the shallots and the rice, and stir until coated in oil, then season with black pepper. Begin to add the hot stock, a ladleful at a time, stirring continuously. Wait for the rice to absorb this before adding any more. Continue until all the stock has been used up and the rice is creamy, about 18–20 minutes.

3 Stir in the whole courgette flowers, and season with some salt, the mint, parsley, butter and Parmesan.

4 Cover for 1 minute to allow the rice to rest, then serve on warm plates and eat at once. Extra Parmesan may be sprinkled on top.

The risotto tastes just as good simply made with young courgettes.

RISOTTO ALLA PARMIGIANA

Parmesan Risotto

This is a good family recipe and one which children love; at least, my nieces and nephews do. It is rich, creamy and flavoursome without being too overpowering.

SERVES 4

100 g (3½ oz) unsalted butter

1 tablespoon olive oil

6 shallots, peeled and finely chopped

sea salt and freshly ground black pepper

350 g (12 oz) *carnaroli* risotto rice

1 litre (1¾ pints) hot, home-made vegetable stock (*see* page 61)

3–4 tablespoons dry white wine

150 g (5½ oz) freshly grated Parmesan

1 Melt the butter and oil in a medium saucepan, add the shallots and some pepper, and fry for 5 minutes until softened.

2 Add the rice and stir well to coat in oil and butter. Now add the vegetable stock, ladle by ladle, stirring between each addition, until the rice is tender but firm and the stock is used up. This will take about 18–20 minutes.

3 When the rice is creamy, stir in the wine, some salt and pepper and the Parmesan.

4 Cover and stand for 1 minute to let the rice rest, before serving on hot plates.

Parmigiano Reggiano is the king of Italian cheeses because it is made with the morning milk, which is laden with the highest levels of calcium. (Grana Padano is secondary, as it is made with the evening's milk.) There are very few cases of osteoporosis in Italy, as Parmesan, with its wealth of bone-nourishing calcium, is eaten in large quantities in every household.

RISOTTO AL RADICCHIO

Radicchio Risotto

Most people think of radicchio as bitter, but cooking it in this way makes it become sweeter. It's also very colourful. This recipe came from Madalena Chapello, a family friend; I spent an entire weekend with her, learning how to cook radicchio.

SERVES 4

6 shallots, peeled and finely chopped

85 g (3 oz) unsalted butter

1 tablespoon olive oil

350 g (12 oz) *carnaroli* risotto rice

125 ml (4½ fl oz) medium red wine

400 g (14 oz) Treviso radicchio, shredded

sea salt and freshly ground black pepper

1 litre (1¾ pints) hot, home-made vegetable stock (*see* page 61)

85 g (3 oz) freshly grated Parmesan

a handful of fresh basil, freshly torn

2 tablespoons finely chopped fresh flat-leaf parsley

1 Fry the shallots in half the butter and all the oil until it has slightly coloured, then add the rice and mix well so that the rice is glistening.

2 Add the wine and shredded radicchio, and season with pepper. Add a ladleful of hot stock and stir well until it has been absorbed by the rice. Continue in this way, adding a ladleful of stock at a time, until all the stock is used up, stirring continuously. This should take about 18–20 minutes.

3 Add some salt, the rest of the butter, the Parmesan, basil and parsley. Adjust the seasoning to taste.

4 Cover for 1 minute to allow the rice to rest. Serve at once on hot plates, with extra grated Parmesan if desired.

Radicchio, being a member of the chicory family of vegetables, is easy to digest when it has been cooked. It is available all year round, and tends to have more strength of flavour in the winter.

SUPPLI DI RISO

Deep-fried Risotto with Shallots, Orange Zest and Mozzarella

This recipe is not for a risotto, but risotto rice is cooked in almost exactly the same way, before being flavoured, then formed into little balls and fried. In the south of Italy, we call them *arancini*, or 'little oranges'. We always seem to eat them when travelling on the boat to Sicily.

SERVES 4

800 ml (29 fl oz) home-made
  vegetable stock (*see* page 61)
50 g (2 oz) unsalted butter
275 g (10 oz) *arborio* risotto
  rice
175 g (6 oz) Mozzarella
  cheese, grated or diced
6 shallots, peeled and finely
  chopped
a handful of mixed fresh herbs,
  chopped

grated zest of 1 large unwaxed
  orange
6 tablespoons freshly grated
  Parmesan
sea salt and freshly ground
  black pepper
1 egg
55 g (2 oz) fresh breadcrumbs
6 tablespoons olive oil

1 In a saucepan bring the stock to the boil, then keep it at just below simmering point.

2 Melt the butter in a large saucepan, add the rice and brown for a few minutes. Stir in a ladleful of hot stock and cook until the liquid has been absorbed. Continue doing this until the rice is cooked and all the stock has evaporated, stirring continuously: about 20 minutes.

3 Now add the cheese, shallots, herbs, orange rind, Parmesan, salt and pepper. Mix in and leave to cool.

4 Form the flavoured rice into balls the size of a plum. Beat the egg and dip the rice balls first into the egg and then into the breadcrumbs.

5 Heat the oil in a frying pan and fry the rice balls until golden on all sides. Drain well on kitchen paper and serve hot or cold.

There are many different combinations and fillings for supplí. *For example, the flavoured rice given here can be wrapped around a cube of cheese, or indeed some meat.*

RISOTTO DI SPINACI

Spinach Risotto

This is dedicated to real spinach lovers like me. In Italy spinach appears on the menu at all times of the year, as Italians believe that, eaten daily, it is the essence of good health. We have many ways of enjoying it, as a result, and this recipe is one.

SERVES 4

1 kg (2 lb 4 oz) spinach
6 shallots, peeled and finely chopped
85 g (3 oz) unsalted butter
350 g (12 oz) *arborio* risotto rice
125 ml (2½ fl oz) white wine

sea salt and freshly ground black pepper
1 litre (1¾ pints) hot, home-made vegetable stock (*see* page 61)
freshly grated nutmeg
85 g (3 oz) freshly grated Parmesan

1 Steam the spinach for a few minutes until soft. Drain very thoroughly, squeeze dry and chop finely.

2 Melt half the butter and fry the shallots until softened. Add the rice and stir together for a few minutes, then add the spinach, wine and some black pepper and mix well.

3 Add a ladleful of hot stock, and stir until this has been absorbed by the rice. Continue to add stock, ladleful by ladleful, stirring continuously, until it has all been used up and the rice is creamy.

4 Remove the pan from the heat and stir in the nutmeg, the rest of the butter, some salt and the Parmesan.

5 Cover for 1 minute to allow the rice to rest. Serve at once on hot plates, and add extra Parmesan at the table if desired.

Spinach's iron and calcium are not readily available because of its oxalic acid content, so it is not as nutritious as we have been led to believe. However, being green, it contains Vitamins A and C – and of course it tastes delicious!

RISI E BISI

Risotto with Peas

This recipe has become a speciality of Venice because of the wonderful soil of the Veneto where peas grow in abundance. In the pea season, there is often such a glut that the vendors don't bother to weigh them out but just pour the pods freely into your bag, so as to ensure that you can enjoy them at their very finest and sweetest.

SERVES 4

1 kg (2 lb 4 oz) sweet fresh
    pea pods, young and tender
6 shallots, peeled and finely
    sliced
2 garlic cloves, peeled and
    finely chopped
55 g (2 oz) unsalted butter
2 tablespoons olive oil
a handful of fresh flat-leaf
    parsley, chopped

1 litre (1¾ pints) hot, home-made
    vegetable stock (*see* page 61)
350 g (12 oz) *vialone nano*
    risotto rice
125 ml (4½ fl oz) dry white wine
sea salt and freshly ground
    black pepper
a handful of fresh mint, chopped
55 g (2 oz) freshly grated
    Parmesan

1 Shell and rinse the peas. Fry the shallots and garlic in the butter and oil until lightly coloured, then stir in the parsley, peas and just enough hot stock to barely cover the ingredients. Simmer gently for 2 minutes.

2 Add the rice, wine and some pepper, and stir to coat the rice with this mixture, using a wooden spoon. Now add the stock ladleful by ladleful, stirring well between each addition, until all the stock has been absorbed and the rice is creamy. This should take 18–20 minutes.

3 Stir in some salt, then the mint and Parmesan.

4 Cover for 1 minute to allow the rice to rest, then serve on to warmed plates with extra grated Parmesan if desired.

Because they are green, peas contain rich supplies of Vitamins A and C. They are a stimulant and supply energy. They should be eaten as freshly as possible because, when plucked from the plant, their sugars rapidly convert to starch.

RISOTTO DI FINOCCHIO

Fennel Risotto

The Italians love fennel, and eat it both raw and cooked. Fennel bulbs are male or female: the females are plump with hips, and the males are long and thin. Do choose both in your cooking, as cooked together they support each other as far as flavour is concerned.

SERVES 4–6

500 g (18 oz) fennel bulbs
6 shallots, peeled and finely chopped
85 g (3 oz) unsalted butter
350 g (12 oz) *arborio* risotto rice
sea salt and freshly ground black pepper

1 litre (1¾ pints) hot, home-made vegetable stock (*see* page 61)
finely grated zest of 2 unwaxed lemons
a handful of fresh flat-leaf parsley, finely chopped
85 g (3 oz) freshly grated Parmesan

1 Wash and trim the fennel, removing all the hard external green bits. Cut the fennel into fine even slices.

2 Fry the fennel and shallots in half the butter for about 5 minutes until tender. Add the rice and stir well until it is glistening with butter.

3 Season with pepper only at this point, then gradually add the hot stock, a ladleful at a time, allowing the rice to absorb the liquid before adding more. Keep stirring and adding stock, ladleful by ladleful, until the rice is creamy. This should take about 18–20 minutes.

4 Add some salt, the lemon zest, parsley, remaining butter and the Parmesan.

5 Cover and allow the rice to rest for 1 minute, then stir once more before transferring to a warmed plate. Eat at once.

Fennel often appears on the table at the end of a meal in Italy, and is eaten raw as a digestive. The male fennel is best for this, as it is less fibrous. The alkalinity of fennel aids digestion, helping to metabolise the fat of a rich meal.

FAGIOLI

Dried peas, beans and lentils are known collectively as pulses. Because they are seeds, they are very nutritious, containing everything for the next generation of plants, just as grains do. All pulses are rich in incomplete protein, so the most nutritious way of eating them is with grains, whose amino acids will help to balance those of the pulse. Pulses contain no cholesterol and very little fat, and are good sources of B vitamins, calcium, iron, potassium, magnesium and zinc.

The fresh peas, beans and lentils that become the familiar dried pulses are harvested in late summer. I love to see fresh beans in Italian markets, their speckled and shiny pods bursting with ripe seeds. They are more common in their dried form in Italy as well, and they are enjoyed there throughout the winter months as a source of nutrients when fresh vegetables are less available.

In Italy we have a vast array of pulses: borlotti and cannellini beans, *lenticchie* (lentils), *fave* (broad beans), *ceci* (chick peas) and *piselli* (peas), to name but a few. We enjoy them particularly in the south of Italy. I was brought up on a very varied diet of pulses, mainly due to the fact that southern Italians concentrate on growing vegetables and other crops rather than on rearing animals such as cattle. (Beef and butter, for instance, are much more northern in culinary terms.) My grandmother had a huge store of pulse recipes that I learned from her, and am happy to share with you.

There are some golden rules you must follow in the cooking of pulses, but otherwise they are blissfully straightforward, quick and easy to prepare. First of all, buy your supplies from a shop with a fast turnover, so that you can be sure they are not too old. All pulses – apart from lentils – must be soaked in lots of cold water, at least overnight, in order to rehydrate them. They should then be covered with fresh cold water, brought to the boil and boiled for 10 minutes; this is in order to inactivate potentially toxic substances many pulses contain. Thereafter, continue cooking the pulses – perhaps with some added flavouring, such as a couple of bay leaves and/or a sprig of fresh thyme – for another 40 minutes, at a slow simmer, or until they are tender. Lentils do not require soaking, and they will only need simmering for about 30 minutes. Salt pulses only after cooking; doing so before will toughen the skins.

A handy rule of thumb is that pulses, when cooked, roughly double in volume and weight: so 250g (9oz) dried beans will become roughly 500g (18oz) after cooking. And don't be ashamed to use canned pulses if you haven't got time, or have forgotten, to soak dried beans; simply drain and rinse them, and heat through for a few minutes before using in a recipe.

ZUPPA DELLA NONNA CON LENTICCHIE E PATATE

Grandmother's Lentil and Potato Soup

This brings back a rush of family and childhood memories. It smells so enticing, and its texture is wonderful. The Italians traditionally eat lentils at New Year because they represent money, therefore potential success in the coming year. The best to use are the *lenticchie di Norcia*, tiny green lentils which are very expensive because they are hand-picked. They are also considered holy, because they grow in the sacred land near Assisi.

SERVES 4

10 new potatoes, preferably
    Italian, scrubbed
sea salt and freshly ground
    black pepper
225 g (8 oz) small green lentils
3 tablespoons olive oil
1 x 700 g (1 lb 6 oz) bottle
    tomato passata or 2 x 400 g
    (14 oz) cans chopped tomatoes

2 garlic cloves, peeled and
    crushed
55 g (2 oz) freshly grated
    Parmesan
a handful of fresh flat-leaf
    parsley, chopped

1 Cut the potatoes into even-sized cubes without removing the skins. Put into a medium saucepan and add 900 ml (1½ pints) boiling water. Season with salt and cook for 10 minutes.

2 Add the lentils, oil, tomato passata, pepper and crushed garlic. Bring to the boil, then cover and simmer for 40 minutes. Adjust the seasoning.

3 Serve sprinkled with Parmesan and parsley.

Lentils are 50 per cent carbohydrate, high in fibre, and 25 per cent protein; they also contain a good quantity of iron. If you have the rind of a piece of Parmesan lurking in your fridge, do use it in this soup (or any other soup) as it enriches the flavour. Whoever is served the rind should make a wish! And to make a dried-out piece of Parmesan assume some of its former glory, wrap it overnight in a damp tea towel.

MINESTRA DI CECI E PEPERONI
Chick Pea and Pepper Soup

This is a family soup which is often served in our village, as we produce so many peppers and chick peas. It's colourful, full of flavour and very satisfying.

SERVES 4

250g (9 oz) chick peas
  (*see* page 79)
2 red onions, peeled and
  chopped
2 tablespoons fruity olive oil
2 medium potatoes, peeled
  and diced
3 red peppers, de-seeded and
  cut into strips

1 carrot, peeled and finely
  chopped
3 ripe tomatoes, cut into
  chunks
2 garlic cloves, peeled
sea salt and freshly ground
  black pepper
a handful of fresh flat-leaf
  parsley, finely chopped
extra-virgin olive oil

1 While the chick peas are cooking, fry the onion in the olive oil for a few minutes, then add the potato, peppers, carrot and tomato, along with the garlic and 4 tablespoons of water.

2 Bring to the boil and cook for 15 minutes over a moderate heat, stirring constantly to stop any of the vegetables from sticking

(add a little more water if necessary). Season well.

3 The moment the chick peas are cooked, pour the prepared sauce into them, stirring gently.

4 Serve the soup in bowls sprinkled with parsley and extra-virgin olive oil. You may like to offer some grated Parmesan to sprinkle on top.

Peppers are high in nutrients such as Vitamins A, B and C, E and K. Red peppers contain more Vitamin A – as beta-carotene – than the green. Many people believe that chick peas have a diuretic effect, and that they can energise, preventing tiredness.

MINESTRA DI CECI
E CASTAGNE

Chestnut Soup with Chick Peas

My father really loves this recipe, as he grows chestnuts in Avellino, in Campania. In Minori, my village, we have a torchlight festival at the end of October to celebrate the chestnut harvest. This soup is one of many ways in which we use chestnuts locally.

SERVES 4

200 g (7 oz) dried chick peas
450 g (1 lb) fresh chestnuts
3 celery sticks
4 bay leaves
7 tablespoons olive oil

4 garlic cloves, peeled
sea salt and freshly ground
black pepper
4 slices country-style bread

1 Soak the chick peas in water overnight.

2 Pre-heat the oven to 200°C/ 400°F/gas mark 6.

3 Score the chestnut skins on the outside – cutting into the skin slightly – and put on a baking tray. Cook in the oven for 40 minutes, leave to cool slightly and peel off the thick outer skin, then the inner skin.

4 Meanwhile, drain the soaked chick peas, and put in a large saucepan with 2.5 litres (4½ pints) fresh water. Add the celery, bay leaves and 2 tablespoons of the oil. Bring to the boil and boil vigorously for 10 minutes. Lower the heat and simmer for 40 minutes until the chick peas are tender and the cooking liquid has reduced.

5 Heat the remaining oil in a frying pan and fry the peeled chestnuts and garlic until golden.

6 Remove the bay leaves and celery from the chick-pea soup and stir in the chestnuts, garlic and oil. Season with salt and pepper.

7 Toast the bread slices. Put them in the bottom of a soup tureen and pour over the soup. Leave for 2–3 minutes before serving.

Chestnuts have high levels of carbohydrate, and very little fat. They are totally organic, as the trees are left to grow entirely naturally. Chestnuts can be used as vegetable, meat substitute, a flour for pasta, pastry etc, and in puddings.

JOTA

Bean and Cabbage Soup

This northern dish is eaten for *pranzo*, lunch, with a hunk of bread during the winter months. It's almost mandatory for all Italians to eat lots of beans during the winter as they believe them to be synonymous with health, warmth and energy. Make this soup the day before to allow all the flavours to amalgamate.

SERVES 4

350 g (12 oz) cooked
  cannellini beans
  (*see* page 79)
1 medium fennel bulb,
  chopped
1 onion, peeled and chopped
2 garlic cloves, peeled and
  crushed

1 green cabbage, shredded
4 tablespoons tomato purée
sea salt and freshly ground
  black pepper
2 tablespoons olive oil
a handful of fresh flat-leaf
  parsley, finely chopped

1 When the beans have nearly finished their cooking, stir in the fennel, onion, garlic, cabbbage, tomato purée, salt and pepper, and simmer for 30 minutes or until the beans are tender.

2 Add the olive oil and parsley adjust the seasoning, and serve.

Cabbage contains Vitamins A, B and C; the darker the colour of the leaves, the higher the content of nutrients.

PAPAZOI

Barley and Bean Soup

A Roman soup which I tasted during a long leisurely Sunday lunch at a local restaurant. It was the star of the show, and it took a long quizzing of the chef to persuade him to part with the recipe.

SERVES 6

200 g (7 oz) dried borlotti
   beans
200 g (7 oz) pot barley
2 tablespoons olive oil
2 garlic cloves, peeled and
crushed
2 litres (3½ pints) water or
   home-made vegetable stock
   (*see* page 61)
200 g (7 oz) potatoes, peeled
   and diced

100 g (4 oz) fresh sweetcorn
   kernels, scraped from the
   raw cob
½ handful fresh sage leaves,
   finely chopped
a handful of fresh flat-leaf
   parsley, finely chopped
sea salt and freshly ground
   black pepper

1 Soak the beans and barley, in separate bowls, overnight.

2 Heat the oil in a large pan, and add the garlic and the drained beans and barley. Pour in the water or stock, bring to the boil, and boil for 10 minutes.

3 Lower the heat, add the potatoes, sweetcorn and sage, and cook more gently for 40 minutes.

4 Stir in the parsley, and season well. Serve immediately.

Pot barley is healthier than pearl, as the husk has not been removed. Pot also has a nuttier flavour, and normally needs to be cooked for longer than pearl to soften and release the starches. These are what create the almost viscous texture of cooked barley, not too dissimilar to that of cooked risotto rice.

CIANFOTTA

Italian Bean Hotpot

This warming and colourful stew is synonymous with Tuscany, where the food tends to be of a rich and substantial nature. You can try different combinations of vegetables to create your own hotpot. This is one of my favourites.

SERVES 4

250g (9 oz) cannellini
    beans (*see* page 79)
1 small aubergine, diced
sea salt and freshly ground
    black pepper
4 tablespoons olive oil
1 onion, peeled and chopped
2 garlic cloves, peeled
2 celery sticks, chopped
1 teaspoon fresh rosemary,
    finely chopped

2 yellow peppers, de-seeded
    and diced
2 potatoes, peeled and diced
450g (1 lb) fresh tomatoes,
    diced
½ teaspoon dried chilli-pepper
    flakes
a handful of fresh flat-leaf
    parsley, chopped
a handful of fresh basil, torn

1 While the beans are cooking, degorge the aubergine. Put the cubes into a colander, sprinkle with salt, cover and weight down, and leave for about 15–20 minutes. Rinse the salt off and pat the cubes dry.

2 Heat the olive oil in a medium saucepan, add the onion and allow it to colour, then add the garlic, celery and rosemary. Let these colour for a few minutes as well, then add the remaining vegetables, salt, pepper and chilli.

3 Stir well, cover lightly, and cook over a low heat for 30 minutes. Add the cooked beans and cook for a further 10 minutes.

4 Stir well, and add the parsley and basil away from the heat. Adjust the seasoning, and serve warm.

This could be called the Italian version of ratatouille, but because of the beans and potatoes – double carbohydrate – it's definitely a dish for the bitingly cold Tuscan winters.

MINESTRONE CON RISO
E FAGIOLI

Vegetable Soup with Rice and Beans

In Italy there are a multitude of vegetable soups or minestrone: roughly translated, the word means a 'mixture' or 'hotchpotch'. There are countless ways of mixing good wholesome ingredients in a soup – one for every day of the year – and this is a particular family favourite of mine.

SERVES 4

2 garlic cloves, peeled and chopped

1 celery stick, finely chopped

1 red onion, peeled and sliced

2 tablespoons olive oil

8 ripe, fresh, red tomatoes, skinned

500 g (18 oz) cooked borlotti beans (*see* page 79)

200 g (7 oz) *arborio* risotto rice

½ teaspoon dried chilli-pepper flakes

a handful of fresh flat-leaf parsley, chopped

a handful of fresh mint, chopped

sea salt and freshly ground black pepper

extra-virgin olive oil

1 Sauté the garlic, celery and onion in the olive oil until softened. Add the tomato and simmer for 10 minutes.

2 Pour this sauce over the cooked beans, then add the rice and 450 ml (¾ pint) water, stirring well.

3 Add the chilli, parsley and mint, and cook for 20 minutes until the rice is tender. You will need to add more water if the soup is looking too thick.

4 Season with salt and pepper, and serve with a drizzle of extra-virgin olive oil.

This is a wonderful example of complete protein, the marriage of pulse and grain: beans and rice. It's a dish typical of the north, where people need fuel and energy for the colder weather.

MILLECOSEDDE

Thick Pulse Soup

The texture of this soup is thick and lumpy. I ate enormous quantities of it when I was a student, as it is satisfying, hearty and very economical (just right when your budget is low). The food of Italy is so regional that something similar to millecosedde appears from the top to the toe of the country, in thousands of different variations – roughly the meaning of its name.

SERVES 6

7 tablespoons olive oil

1 carrot, peeled and chopped

1 onion, peeled and chopped

1 garlic clove, peeled and finely chopped

2 litres (3½ pints) home-made vegetable stock (*see* page 61)

½ small cabbage, blanched and shredded

200g (7 oz) cooked borlotti beans (*see* page 79)

200g (7 oz) cooked haricot or cannellini beans

200g (7 oz) cooked chick peas

100g (4 oz) cooked green lentils

225g (8 oz) mushrooms, finely sliced

sea salt and freshly ground black pepper

225g (8 oz) farfalle (bows) or other small pasta shapes

100g (4 oz) freshly grated Pecorino cheese,

a handful of fresh flat-leaf parsley, finely chopped

1 Heat the oil in a large heavy pan, add the carrot, onion and garlic, and fry gently for 5 minutes.

2 Add the stock and bring to the boil, then lower the heat, add the cabbage and simmer for 5 minutes.

3 Add the drained pulses to the cabbage pan with the mushrooms, salt and pepper.

4 Stir well, add the pasta, and cook for a further 10 minutes.

5 Sprinkle with cheese and parsley to serve.

INSALATA DI FAGIOLI DELLA NONNA

Grandmother's Bean Salad

As Italian bread goes stale so quickly, we have an infinite number of recipes which use it up. This is a typical southern recipe with the hint of piquant heat so prevalent in the south.

SERVES 4

250g (9 oz) cooked cannellini
   beans (*see* page 79)
zest of 1 unwaxed lemon
6 tablespoons extra-virgin
   olive oil
2 tablespoons red wine
   vinegar

½ teaspoon dried chilli-pepper
   flakes
a handful of mixed fresh herbs
   (parsley, thyme and oregano)
100g (3½ oz) country bread,
   cut into small cubes
sea salt and freshly ground
   black pepper

1 Drain the beans, and leave to cool.

2 Mix the remaining ingredients apart from the bread and seasoning, and add to the cooled beans.

3 Add the bread, mix in, and adjust the seasoning. Serve immediately.

The combination of bread (grain) and pulse here enables the dish to be a complete source of protein.

PURE DI FAVE CON CICORIA

Chicory with Cannellini Bean Purée

In Italy there are several types of chicory: Belgian chicory, frizzy *frisée*, *endive*, *batavia* and the radicchios all belong to the chicory family. They are bitter in flavour, and marry well with the comparative sweetness of the beans. You may like to cook the chicory first: blanch it only, so that it remains *al dente*, or brush with olive oil and grill as for radicchio.

SERVES 4

200 g (7 oz) cooked cannellini beans (*see page 79*)

1 garlic clove, peeled and crushed

2 tablespoons extra-virgin olive oil

2 teaspoons fresh marjoram, chopped

1 tablespoon lemon juice

grated zest of 1 unwaxed lemon

sea salt and freshly ground black pepper

2 Belgian chicory heads

25 g (1 oz) black olives, pitted

a small handful of fresh flat-leaf parsley, chopped

1 Heat the cooked cannellini beans gently in a medium saucepan.

2 Mash the beans with a potato masher, along with the garlic. Then stir in the olive oil, marjoram, lemon juice and zest. Season to taste.

3 Wash and dry the chicory leaves. Divide them between four plates and arrange the warm purée on the leaves. Serve garnished with the olives and parsley.

A good balance of flavours, the bitter and the sweet, and a good balance of nutrients too. I like to keep a bean purée in the fridge for snacking and nibbling purposes. (They improve with age, but don't keep longer than two days.)

INSALATA DEL CONTADINO
Farmer's Salad

Once, when I was walking in the fields surrounding the cookery school, I asked a couple of the workers what they had for lunch, and it turned out to be this salad. Broccoli is grown locally in Umbria, although it is generally regarded as a southern Italian vegetable, appearing in the cooler months of the year.

SERVES 4

250 g (9 oz) cooked borlotti
    beans (*see* page 79)
4 tablespoons extra-virgin
    olive oil
3 tablespoons lemon juice
½ teaspoon dried chilli-pepper
    flakes

sea salt and freshly ground
    black pepper
500 g (18 oz) broccoli florets
a handful of fresh flat-leaf
    parsley, finely chopped

1 Make the dressing first. In a serving dish large enough to hold the beans and broccoli, mix the extra-virgin olive oil, lemon juice, chilli, salt and pepper.

2 Place the broccoli in a large pan of boiling salted water, and cook until *al dente*. Drain and pour into the dish with the dressing.

3 Add the cooked beans and parsley and mix well. Serve at room temperature.

A vitamin-C-enriched salad. Adding a little olive oil to the cooking water when boiling green vegetables helps them to retain their colour.

TORTINO

Layered Courgette and Barley Bake

Barley is known as *orzo* in Italy, and makes a nutritious and wholesome meal served with crusty bread, followed by a crisp green salad. I hope this will become part of your weekly repertoire: it's real comfort food, eaten like a risotto. An ancient grain, a type of spelt (a species of wheat), known as *farro*, is also grown in Italy and is used in similar ways.

SERVES 4

225 g (8 oz) pearl barley

1 litre (1¾ pints) Vegetable Stock (*see* page 61)

3 tablespoons olive oil

55 g (2 oz) butter

450 g (1 lb) courgettes, topped, tailed and sliced

2 garlic cloves, peeled and crushed

6 ripe tomatoes, chopped

150 g (5½ oz) Mozzarella cheese, diced

sea salt and freshly ground black pepper

a handful of fresh basil, torn

a handful of fresh mint, chopped

a handful of fresh flat-leaf parsley, chopped

100 g (3½ oz) freshly grated Parmesan

55 g (2 oz) fresh white bread crumbs

1 In a large saucepan, cook the barley in the vegetable stock for 25 minutes until most of the stock has been absorbed.

2 Pre-heat the oven to 200° C / 400° F / gas mark 6.

3 Heat the oil and butter in a frying pan, add the courgette and garlic, and fry until golden. Drain and reserve.

4 Add the tomato and Mozzarella to the barley with the salt, pepper, basil, mint, parsley and grated Parmesan.

5 To assemble, arrange half the courgette in a shallow ovenproof dish in a neat layer. Now add all the barley mixture and then a neat layer of the remaining sliced courgette.

6 Spread the breadcrumbs over, then bake for 20 minutes until golden brown.

Italians make a drink with barley – called bimbo *– which has energy-giving properties, and is good for children and infants because it is easy to digest. Barley water is considered to be nutritive in Britain as well.*

FAGIOLINI E PATATE CON PESTO

Beans with Potatoes and Pesto

A wonderful way of enjoying pesto, rather than on pasta, which seems to be the most common usage. These three ingredients together produce something rather memorable.

SERVES 4

Pesto

3 garlic cloves, peeled

85 g (3 oz) fresh basil leaves

4 tablespoons extra-virgin olive oil

3 tablespoons freshly grated Parmesan

1 tablespoon freshly grated Pecorino Romano cheese

2 tablespoons pine kernels

250 g (9 oz) cooked cannellini beans (*see* page 79)

250 g (9 oz) Italian new potatoes, scrubbed and quartered (*Spunto* is a good variety)

sea salt and freshly ground black pepper

1 Start by making the pesto. I firmly believe in making pesto by hand in a large pestle and mortar. First, crush the garlic, then add the basil leaves plus the oil, and grind to a paste. Add the cheeses and pine kernels, and grind to your desired texture.

2 Drain the beans. Cook the potatoes until tender, then drain well.

3 Add the potatoes to the beans. Pour in the pesto and mix well. Adjust the seasoning if needed.

Pesto made painstakingly by hand is infinitely superior to throwing your ingredients into a food processor and letting it do all the work. The oils in the basil are released more slowly if you work by hand, so the flavour is better. In a food processor, there seems to be some chemical reaction between basil and garlic and the stainless-steel blade, which gives a metallic taste to the pesto. We've actually made a direct comparison at the cookery school, tasting one pesto against another, and the hand-pounded one wins every time.

CROSTINI DI LENTICCHIE

Lentil Crostini

This appears on every menu in Umbria, and often will come as part of a mixed
plate of crostini, along with a meat purée and a vegetable one. Although made
with humble ingredients, the crostini can be served as an elegant starter for a
dinner party. The best lentils to use are the *lenticchie di Norcia* (*see* page 81).

SERVES 4

Lentil Purée

1 tablespoon olive oil

1 small onion, peeled and very
   finely chopped

4–5 fresh sage leaves, finely
   chopped

225 g (8 oz) small green lentils

500 ml (18 fl oz) boiling water

sea salt and freshly ground
   black pepper

To serve

8 slices slightly stale country
   bread, toasted

a few fresh sage leaves, finely
   chopped

1 To make the purée, put the oil in a saucepan and heat for 2 minutes. Add the onion and sage, and sauté for 5 minutes.

2 Add the lentils and, as soon as they are well coated with oil, pour over the boiling water.

3 Cover and simmer for about 1 hour or until the lentils are soft but still whole. Season with salt and pepper.

4 Spread while warm on to the toast slices, and garnish with the chopped sage leaves.

Crostini are very popular in Italy because we always have so much stale bread left over. This is because, when salt tax was imposed – around the twelfth century – bakers decided not to use it, and of course bread without salt goes stale very quickly. In fact, in my village, we have to buy bread twice a day.

FAGIOLI ALL'UCCELLETTO
Beans with Tomato Sauce and Sage

This is a typical dish from Tuscany. Its name is derived from *uccelletti* or 'little birds', as the sage leaves resemble little birds' beaks. Another way of enjoying sage is to dip leaves into flour, then eggs beaten with grated Parmesan, then to fry them until they resemble golden pillows. Serve as an appetiser with drinks.

SERVES 4

50 ml (2 fl oz) olive oil

25 g (1 oz) unsalted butter

3 garlic cloves, peeled and crushed

12 fresh sage leaves, roughly chopped

½ x 400 g (14 oz) can chopped tomatoes, or 6 ripe tomatoes, chopped

250 g (9 oz) cooked cannellini beans (*see* page 79)

sea salt and freshly ground black pepper

extra-virgin olive oil

1 Heat the olive oil and butter in a saucepan. Add the garlic and sage and fry gently for 1 minute.

2 Add the tomatoes and cooked beans, then season with salt and pepper and simmer for 15 minutes.

3 Serve hot with extra-virgin olive oil drizzled on top.

You can burn sage leaves in your home, for cleansing purposes, and for encouraging clarity of mind with less forgetfulness! The name of the herb in English comes from the word meaning wise.

FARINATA

Chick Pea Bake

If you keep some chick-pea flour in your store cupboard, this recipe can be a real standby. It makes an interesting accompaniment to other foods – meats or vegetables – and may be pepped up by herbs, more garlic and pehaps some chilli. Use your culinary licence and experiment!

SERVES 4

1½ litres (2¾ pints) home-made
    vegetable stock
    (*see* page 61) or water
450g (1 lb) chick-pea flour

sea salt and freshly ground
    black pepper
2 garlic cloves, peeled and
    crushed
6–8 tablespoons olive oil

1 Pour the stock or water into a heavy large pan, then gradually stir in the flour. Add some salt and the garlic, and cook over a gentle heat for 1 hour, stirring frequently and skimming the surface with a slotted spoon occasionally. It should be smooth and quite thick.

2 Meanwhile, pre-heat the oven to 200°C/400°F/gas mark 6.

3 Pour the mixture into an oiled roasting pan and level the surface. Sprinkle the oil over the top. Bake in the pre-heated oven for 30 minutes until golden brown. Sprinkle liberally with pepper, and serve immediately.

The French have a similar dish called panisse, *also made with chick pea flour. This flour is also used in the Indian sub-continent, where it is known as* gram *or* besan, *and is used in the making of many batters and noodles.*

VERDURA

When I am travelling through Italy, mainly by train, it always makes me happy to see back and front gardens, station flower beds, window boxes and terracotta pots on sunny balconies brimming with bushy tomato plants or rows of basil or oregano. Around midday, you might be lucky enough to catch a glimpse of the cook's deft hand reaching out of a window to pinch a sprig of fresh basil to add savour to her spaghetti.

This brings home to me, every time, the fact that the Italians were the original market gardeners. Many of the vegetables we are familiar with today were developed in Italy, among them tomatoes, broccoli, fennel, celery and artichokes. The land is still principally utilised for growing, much more than it is for grazing, and as a result the Italians have always been much more interested in vegetables as food and inventive with vegetable recipes. Meat is seen as an expensive commodity, and its consumption in Italy is much less than that in many other Western countries. Vegetables are so important to the Italians, in fact, that they have been given a course in the meal all of their own: *contorno*.

The quality of vegetables in Italy is superb, as they are grown for flavour rather than for looks or for quantity – and I am not just saying that because my father is a vegetable grower (amongst many other things)! How I wish that Italian varieties of potato, onion, courgette and pepper were more widely available in Britain, where I live. They just simply taste so much better, and I'm sure would do us more good, as vegetables grown in Italy tend to be entirely organic.

When it is harvest time, vegetables are treated and cooked very carefully. They are never drowned in a lot of water, or boiled for a great length of time because this would deprive them of their vitamins. Rather, they are steamed or poached briefly in the minimum of water, or sautéed briskly in some wonderful olive oil with complementary flavourings such as garlic, shallot and/or chilli. Green vegetables are added to boiling water with a teaspoon of olive oil which helps preserve their vibrant colour, and a saucepan lid is never used as this would also cause the colour to fade. The cooking water from vegetables is always reserved and used for soups the next day: a healthy practice, as the water contains any nutrients leached from the vegetables.

The recipes in this chapter contain a number of influences, from both north and south. The warmer south is where Mediterranean vegetables, such as tomatoes, peppers, courgettes and aubergines flourish, and the local recipes reflect this bounty. Many of the vegetables which are more familiar to those in northern Europe, such as cauliflower, are grown in the colder north.

ZUCCHINI A SCAPECE

Sun-dried Courgettes with Mint and Garlic

This can be eaten either as a vegetable dish on its own, or as a salad; perfect with some good bread. When I make it at the school, we tend to eat it straight away, but the marinading intensifies the flavours. The longer it is left, the stronger it will be, but it is so good you won't be able to leave it for very long. I suggest you double the quantities right from the beginning.

SERVES 6

9 large courgettes, topped and tailed

175 ml (6 fl oz) olive oil

a large handful of fresh mint leaves, coarsely chopped

3 garlic cloves, peeled and finely chopped

6 tablespoons good-quality white-wine vinegar

4 tablespoons extra-virgin olive oil

sea salt

1 Cut the courgettes into thin slices lengthways. Place them on a wooden board, cover with a cloth and leave them in the sun to dry for about 3 hours. Alternatively, put them on a baking sheet in the oven at 140°C/275°F/gas mark 1 for about an hour to dry out completely without colouring.

2 Heat the olive oil in a large pan and fry all the dried courgette slices, in batches if necessary, until golden. Don't bother to turn them over. Drain carefully on kitchen paper.

3 Transfer the courgette slices to a dish and sprinkle with the mint, garlic, vinegar, extra-virgin olive oil and salt. Cover and leave to stand for about 4 hours in a cool place or, even better, overnight.

This method of 'cooking', called a scapece, is very Neapolitan, and it is often applied to fish such as sardines as well as vegetables. Aubergine and strips of sweet pepper can be prepared in the same way.

FAVE CON CIPOLLA ROSSA E FORMAGGIO

Broad Beans Sautéed with Red Onion and Goat's Cheese

In the restaurant of a smart hotel outside Rome, I asked if they had broad beans on the menu. Moments later arrived a beautiful platter covered with chunks of ice on which were arranged sheaves of fresh broad beans in the pod. This is how most Italians enjoy broad beans: raw. However, cooking them is also delicious.

SERVES 4

1 kg (2 lb 4 oz) broad beans in the
   pod, podded and skinned
1 medium red onion, peeled
   and chopped
2 tablespoons olive oil

1 x 200 g (7 oz) packet
   goat's cheese
sea salt and freshly ground
   black pepper
paprika

1 Boil or steam the podded and skinned broad beans until tender: about 10 minutes.

2 Sauté the onion in the olive oil for about 5 minutes, then add the hot drained beans, and season to taste. Mix well.

3 Serve in a dish, with thinly sliced goat's cheese in a stripe across the top. Sprinkle with paprika.

Skinning broad beans to reveal their bright green inner kernels is immensely time-consuming – and rather uneconomical – but it produces a sweeter, much more texturally interesting and visually exciting broad bean.

FAVE AL VINO

Broad Beans with a Wine Sauce

On every street corner in the spring you can see groups of little old men passing the time eating young broad beans straight from the pod. This recipe is a way to use broad beans when they are not so young and tender, and cannot be eaten raw.

SERVES 4

1 kg (2 lb 4 oz) broad beans in the pod

25 g (1 oz) butter

½ onion, peeled and finely chopped

25 g (1 oz) plain flour

1 sprig fresh marjoram, chopped

sea salt and freshly ground black pepper

1 teaspoon caster sugar

300 ml (½ pint) white wine

150 ml (¼ pint) home-made vegetable stock (*see* page 61)

1 Shell the broad beans.

2 Put the butter in a pan with the finely chopped onion, and cook for 4 minutes until golden. Stir in the flour, and cook until you have a thick roux: about 1 minute.

3 Add the beans and the marjoram, salt and pepper, sugar and white wine, and mix all together.

4 Add the stock, mix and simmer gently for 20–25 minutes until the beans are tender.

Being green, fresh broad beans contain good levels of Vitamin C. You may prefer to remove the outer greyish skin of the beans to reveal the bright green kernels underneath.

MELANZANE CON FUNGHETTI

Aubergine with Tomato and Garlic Sauce

The aubergine is related to the tomato and potato. There are male and female aubergines, as in most of the plant kingdom. The male can be identified by a concave base and, when cut into, has fewer seeds. As a result, the male has a better flavour, because the seeds can be bitter.

SERVES 4

1 large aubergine, cut into
   2½ cm (1 in) cubes
sea salt and freshly ground
   black pepper
150 ml (¼ pint) olive oil
2 garlic cloves, peeled and
   crushed

350 g (12 oz) tomatoes, skinned
   and chopped
1 tablespoon salted capers,
   rinsed and drained

1 Put the aubergine in a colander, sprinkle lightly with salt, cover, weight down and leave to stand for half an hour. Rinse the aubergine under cold running water, then drain and dry thoroughly.

2 Heat the oil in a heavy pan, add the garlic and fry gently until coloured.

3 Add the aubergine and fry for 10 minutes, then add the tomatoes, capers and salt and pepper to taste. Cover and simmer for 30–40 minutes, stirring occasionally. Serve hot or cold.

Capers are the flower bud of a shrub native to the Mediterranean. They are available pickled in brine, or salted. The latter are far superior in flavour but, because the buds will have absorbed much of the salt, they need to be thoroughly rinsed before use. Capers in balsamic vinegar and caper buds can occasionally be found.

SCAFATA

Broad Beans with Swiss Chard and Tomato

This is from Piedmont, in the north of Italy, and it is traditionally made with *bietli da taglio*, very young Swiss chard leaves. However, if this is not available, spinach will do.

SERVES 4

4 tablespoons olive oil, fruity
  and good quality
1 garlic clove, peeled and
  crushed
1 onion, peeled and chopped
1 carrot, peeled and diced
1 celery stick, diced
750g (1 lb 10 oz) fresh broad
  beans in the pod, podded
sea salt and freshly ground
  black pepper

450g (1 lb) tender Swiss chard,
  ribs discarded, leaves cut
  into strips
450g (1 lb) tomatoes, skinned,
  seeded and finely chopped
a handful of fresh flat-leaf
  parsley, chopped
a handful of fresh mint, chopped
extra-virgin olive oil

1 Warm the oil in a large saucepan, than add the garlic, onion, carrot, celery and beans, and stir-fry for a few minutes. Add salt and pepper and 4 tablespoons water, cover and cook over a very low heat until the beans are tender. This will depend on their size: if they are young and tender, they will only take about 5–7 minutes. If the mixture becomes too dry, add more water.

2 Add the chard leaves and tomato, and cook with the lid partly on until the tomato thickens and the water evaporates.

3 Add the parsley and mint, and adjust the seasoning. I like this dish served just warm with some extra-virgin olive oil drizzled on top.

Chard and spinach, being dark green in colour, are rich in Vitamins A and C, and iron. Cook for the least possible time to preserve the C content.

SPINACI ALLA ROMANA

Spinach with Raisins and Pine Kernels

Alla romana means cooking in the style of Rome. The Romans are very inventive, and this recipe is typical, with pine kernels and raisins to boost the basic flavours of spinach, oil and garlic. Not everyone likes the combination of sweet with savoury, but this is really interesting and flavourful.

SERVES 4

1 kg (2 lb 4 oz) spinach, tough
   stalks removed
2 tablespoons olive oil
25 g (1 oz) butter
1 garlic clove, peeled and sliced
25 g (1 oz) pine kernels

25 g (1 oz) seedless raisins,
   soaked in lukewarm water
   for 15 minutes and drained
sea salt and freshly ground
   black pepper

1 Wash the spinach, then cook in a large pan, with only the water clinging to the leaves, until just tender. Drain well and squeeze out any excess water.

2 Heat the oil and butter in a heavy pan and add the garlic. Fry gently until lightly coloured, then discard the garlic.

3 Add the spinach to the fragrant oil along with the pine kernels and drained raisins. Cook for 10 minutes, stirring frequently, then add salt and pepper to taste. Serve hot.

Any green leaf is high in Vitamins A and C. Dried fruits are a source of nutrients, and the pine kernels, like all nuts, contain many essential fatty acids.

ZUCCA ALL'AGRODOLCE DI PALERMO

Sweet and Sour Pumpkin

I adore pumpkin. This is a typical Sicilian dish, using a sweet spice in a savoury context. Many Sicilian recipes utilise a combination of spices, nuts and dried fruits, an influence from the island's Byzantine past.

SERVES 4

1 kg (2 lb 4 oz) pumpkin, peeled and de-seeded

5 tablespoons olive oil

1 garlic clove, peeled and left whole

1 tablespoon granulated sugar

a handful of fresh mint leaves, chopped

a pinch of powdered cinnamon

8 tablespoons white-wine vinegar

freshly ground black pepper

1 Cut the pumpkin flesh into slices roughly 1 cm (½ in) thick. Fry in hot oil with the whole garlic clove for about 3 minutes. Discard the garlic as soon as it colours.

2 When all the pumpkin slices are fried, place them all back together in the pan, draining off the superfluous oil. Take off the heat.

3 Dredge with sugar, chopped mint and cinnamon. Mix well, then pour the vinegar over, add pepper to taste, cover with the lid, and leave to infuse. Serve warm or cold.

Pumpkins, being yellow fleshed, are rich in beta-carotene, vegetable Vitamin A. If you save the seeds, you can dry them in a low oven and eat them as a snack – they are full of zinc (particularly good for men).

CARCIOFI CON SPINACI

Artichoke Hearts with Spinach

In Italy, artichokes are sold along the roadside from lorries during the artichoke season, which is April, May and October. This recipe comes from the Marche region, famous for delicious artichokes, as well as spinach.

SERVES 4

6 tablespoons olive oil

1 small onion, peeled and finely chopped

1 garlic clove, peeled and crushed

1 kg (2 lb 4 oz) spinach, washed, drained and finely chopped

25 g (1 oz) plain flour

sea salt and freshly ground black pepper

8 young globe artichokes

50 g (2 oz) dried breadcrumbs

50 g (2 oz) freshly grated Parmesan

a handful of fresh mint, finely chopped

a handful of fresh flat-leaf parsley, chopped

1 Heat half the oil in a large heavy pan, add the onion and garlic, and fry gently for 5 minutes. Add the spinach and cook for 2 minutes.

2 Stir in the flour and salt and pepper to taste, cover and cook gently for 5 minutes.

3 Pre-heat the oven to 200°C / 400°F / gas mark 6.

4 Clean the artichokes, discarding the hard outer leaves, spikes and chokes (*see* below). Stand them close together in an oiled ovenproof dish then cover with the spinach.

5 Scatter with the remaining oil, the breadcrumbs, Parmesan, pepper and mint. Bake in the pre-heated oven for 20 minutes, then sprinkle with parsley and serve.

Try to buy young artichokes with long, uncut stems. The shorter the stem, the more tough the artichoke tends to be. In young artichokes, the choke will not have developed very much; to remove what 'fluff' there might be present, spread the top leaves, reach in with a teaspoon, and scrape.

CARCIOFI ALLE MANDORLE

Artichoke Hearts with Almond Sauce

This dish is enjoyed in Calabria in the artichoke season, using fresh hearts, but as these are rather hard to come by, you can use tinned. Calabrian dishes are sweet-sour, and use a lot of almonds, exhibiting the influence of North Africa.

SERVES 4

6 canned artichoke hearts, drained

2 tablespoons capers, chopped (optional)

2 small pickled gherkins, chopped (optional)

Almond sauce

½ red onion, peeled and grated

4 tablespoons olive oil

1 garlic clove, peeled and crushed

100 g (4 oz) ground almonds

300 ml (½ pint) light home-made vegetable stock (*see* page 61)

1 tablespoon white-wine vinegar

1 tablespoon caster sugar

juice of 1 lemon

sea salt and freshly ground black pepper

1 For the sauce, fry the onion until golden in 1 tablespoon of the oil, then add the garlic, and allow to colour lightly. Then add the almonds and the stock, and simmer for about 15 minutes until thick and creamy.

2 Beat in the remaining oil, the vinegar, sugar, lemon juice and a little salt and pepper, adjusting the quantities to taste. Leave to cool.

3 Arrange the artichoke hearts on individual plates, pour the sauce over them, and garnish if liked with capers and pickled gherkins. Serve cold.

The almond sauce is wonderfully creamy, and can be served not just with artichokes but with any other cooked vegetable. As it is completely wheat and dairy free, it is ideal for those with allergies.

POMODORI AL FORNO

Oven-baked Tomatoes

I invented this recipe when at home in Italy, to use up a glut of tomatoes. It's great made ahead of time and re-heated, but it's good cold as well.

SERVES 4

4 large fresh plum tomatoes
unsalted butter
100 g (3½ oz) cooked broccoli,
    chopped
125 g (4½ oz) Provolone cheese,
    diced
2 tablespoons olive oil

½ garlic clove, peeled and
    crushed
100 g (3½ oz) fresh breadcrumbs
a handful of fresh flat-leaf
    parsley, finely chopped
sea salt and freshly ground
    black pepper

1 Core the tomatoes and cut them in half lengthways. Gently squeeze out some of the juice and pulp. Trim a small piece off the bottom of each tomato so it will sit without tilting.

2 Place the cut halves in a buttered baking dish large enough to hold them in a single layer. Set to one side.

3 Pre-heat the oven to 180° C / 350° F / gas mark 4.

4 In a bowl combine the broccoli and cheese. In a frying pan heat the oil and sauté the garlic lightly. Add the breadcrumbs and parsley, and mix well. Add the breadcrumb mixture to the broccoli and cheese, and season with salt and pepper.

5 Divide the broccoli mixture evenly between the tomato halves. Bake the tomatoes until the cheese is bubbly and the crumbs begin to brown: about 20 minutes. Serve immediately.

The broccoli and cheese filling could also be used to stuff courgettes, aubergines and onions (the latter would need to be blanched and hollowed out first, see page 135).

INVOLTINI DI MELANZANE
Aubergine Bundles

Involtini are 'little rolls', and can be made with many other ingredients: for instance Ricotta in place of the Mozzarella. The rolls are like aubergine sandwiches, and would be ideal for an antipasto or starter.

SERVES 4

1 medium aubergine
sea salt and freshly ground
    black pepper
6 tablespoons olive oil
1 red pepper, roasted and
    skinned (*see* below)

225 g (8 oz) Mozzarella cheese,
    sliced lengthways
a handful of fresh basil leaves

1 Wash the aubergine and cut off the stem end. Slice lengthways into 5 mm-(¼ in-)thick slices: you should have about 12. Layer the slices in a colander, sprinkling salt between each layer. Cover, weight down and allow to stand for about half an hour. Then rinse and pat dry.

2 In a frying pan, heat half the oil, and sauté the aubergine slices in batches, keeping them limp, ie not overcooking them, as they will become too brown and will crack. Drain the aubergine slices on kitchen paper.

3 Pre-heat the oven to 200°C / 400°F / gas mark 6.

4 Lay each slice of aubergine on a flat surface. Divide the roasted pepper into the same number of portions as you have aubergine slices. Place a portion of pepper on each aubergine slice. Add a slice of Mozzarella and a basil leaf, then season each slice with salt and pepper.

5 Roll each aubergine slice up into a cylinder. Place in a lightly oiled roasting tin and cover the dish with foil.

6 Heat through in the pre-heated oven for 10 minutes.

The most successful way to roast a pepper is to place it whole in a roasting tin in an oven pre-heated to 200°C / 400°F / gas mark 6 for 25 minutes. Remove the pepper from the oven and let it cool completely before gently peeling off the skin. Enclosing the pepper in a bag before skinning – as many recipes advise – creates too much steam: the pepper flesh becomes too watery and thus has less texture.

CIPOLLINE IN AGRODOLCE

Sweet and Sour Onions

This is a typical antipasto dish which is eaten throughout the whole of Italy. It makes a good preserve, covered with olive oil in jars. Of all the dishes I cook at the school, this, one of the simplest, gets the most compliments. It's also a great way of using up the over-abundance of grapes in September and October: in fact, for the photograph, we picked bunches of sweet and succulent grapes straight from the vines around the school, brought them back to the kitchen, halved them and tossed them immediately in the juices of the onions. Nothing could be more delicious.

Bortonni onions are small and flat, similar to a disc in shape. Native to Italy, they can be quite hard to find elsewhere, but shallots or large spring/salad onions will substitute very well.

SERVES 4

1 dessertspoon caster sugar

15 g (½ oz) butter

2 bay leaves

450 g (1 lb) Italian *bortonni* onions or shallots, peeled

50 ml (2 fl oz) white wine

sea salt and freshly ground black pepper

100 g (3½ oz) black grapes, halved and de-seeded

a handful of fresh flat-leaf parsley, chopped (optional)

1 Heat the sugar in a heavy pan with a tablespoon of water until it caramelises and becomes the colour of hay. Immediately stir in the butter and bay leaves.

2 Toss the onions in this mixture for a couple of minutes, then pour in the wine. Season, bring to the boil, cover and simmer for 20 minutes.

3 Add the grapes and simmer for a further 10 minutes, with the lid off, to reduce the liquid. Adjust the seasoning and remove the bay leaves.

4 Pour into a dish and garnish with parsley if liked. Serve hot or cold.

Shallots and onions (and garlic) all contain sulphurous chemicals called allins, which are responsible for the onion odour (as well as the tears induced by cutting onions). These are believed by traditional medicine to be tonic, stimulant and diuretic.

FAGIOLI IN PADELLA

'Ratatouille' of French Beans

This is a speciality of Domodossola, an area in Lombardy in the north of Italy. It is a really tasty bean recipe, and even better made the day before as all the flavours will have mingled together. I like it as a simple meal served with crusty bread and a salad to follow.

SERVES 4

900 g (2 lb) French beans
2 tablespoons olive oil
1 small onion, peeled and
  chopped
2 garlic cloves, peeled and
  crushed
2 tablespoons fresh flat-leaf
  parsley, finely chopped

1 teaspoon fresh basil or
  ¼ teaspoon dried basil
50 ml (2 fl oz) dry red wine
225 g (8 oz) canned tomatoes
  and their juices, chopped
sea salt and freshly ground
  black pepper

1 Top and tail the beans, and cut them into 5 cm (2 in) lengths.

2 Heat the olive oil in a large frying pan and cook the onion, garlic, parsley and basil for 3 minutes.

3 Add the red wine and cook over a moderate heat until the wine has almost evaporated.

4 Add the beans and tomatoes, season to taste with salt and pepper, and cook gently for 30 minutes or until the beans are tender and the sauce has thickened. Serve hot.

In the north of Italy, people use more alcohol in their cooking than is used in the south. It adds flavour and is a great booster to the beans – and the body! Always use wine that you would drink; please don't compromise on quality, cooking with cheap wines.

CAVOLFIORI DI AMALFI

Parmesan-fried Cauliflower

This is a family recipe, which can be made with broccoli as well. Do try it, as it will change the face and flavour of cauliflower for you. Cauliflower cheese will never be the same again!

SERVES 4

1 medium cauliflower
2 tablespoons plain flour
2 free-range eggs
4 tablespoons freshly grated
   Parmesan

sea salt and freshly ground
   black pepper
a good handful of fresh flat-leaf
   parsley
6 tablespoons olive oil

1 Break the cauliflower into florets, then steam for 6 minutes until tender. Leave to cool completely.

2 Coat the cauliflower florets in flour, one at a time.

3 Beat the eggs, then add the Parmesan, salt and pepper. Finely chop most of the parsley and add it as well.

4 Dip the florets in the egg mixture.

5 Heat the oil in a frying pan and, when hot, shallow-fry the cauliflower florets until golden brown on all sides. Drain and serve hot, cold or warm, scattered with the remaining parsley leaves.

Make sure the cauliflower is absolutely cold, otherwise the batter won't stick. When steaming any brassica, breaking up some bay leaves in the water will neutralise the smell, adding the bay's own aroma at the same time.

PEPERONI E PORCINI

Sweet Peppers and Porcini

My naughty friend Claudio gave me this recipe. He has a restaurant called La Taverna in Perugia. This dish is always on his menu, and it is always cooked to perfection.

SERVES 4

75 g (3 oz) dried *porcini* mushrooms, reconstituted (*see* page 32)

2 tablespoons olive oil

2 garlic cloves, peeled and finely chopped

2 red peppers, de-seeded and thinly sliced

1 yellow pepper, de-seeded and thinly sliced

1 medium fennel bulb, thinly sliced

sea salt and freshly ground black pepper

1 Drain the porcini in a sieve, reserving 2 tablespoons of their soaking water. Dice the *porcini*.

2 In a heavy-based medium saucepan, heat the olive oil and sauté the garlic until soft but not too coloured.

3 Add the sliced peppers and the fennel, and sauté for 5 minutes, then add the porcini and the reserved porcini soaking water.

4 Cover the saucepan, and simmer for 5 minutes. Season with salt and pepper, and serve at once.

Never throw away porcini *soaking water as it contains so much concentrated flavour. I use it as stock, in soups, sauces and risottos.*

PEPERONATA

Peppers with Tomato and Onion

This is a classic pepper dish from the south of Italy, where peppers grow in profusion. I should think every household has its own 'blend'. If you put the peperonata in a jar with olive oil to cover, it makes a wonderful present.

SERVES 4

6 tablespoons olive oil

1 onion, peeled and sliced

1 garlic clove, peeled and sliced

2 large red and 2 large yellow peppers, de-seeded and cut into strips

sea salt and freshly ground black pepper

350g (12 oz) tomatoes, skinned and chopped

a handful of fresh flat-leaf parsley, finely chopped

1 Heat the oil in a heavy pan, add the onion and garlic, and cook gently for 5 minutes.

2 Add the peppers, and salt and pepper to taste. Cook for a further 5 minutes, stirring occasionally.

3 Add the tomatoes and parsley to the peppers. Adust the seasoning, cover and simmer for 20–30 minutes, stirring frequently until thickened. Serve hot or cold as an antipasto.

Peppers are rich in Vitamin C, as are tomatoes and parsley. Green peppers are unripe and therefore not so sweet as the fully ripe red or yellow peppers. Generally speaking, green peppers are not used much in Italian cooking.

ZUCCHINI CON ANICE

Courgettes with Aniseed

As soon as I see courgettes in the shops, I know summer is near. Friends in the Veneto gave me this recipe. Usually I cook courgettes with mint, but was very pleasantly surprised to taste how good they are with aniseed.

SERVES 4

2 tablespoons best-quality olive oil

2 garlic cloves, peeled and finely minced

½ teaspoon dried chilli-pepper flakes

4 medium courgettes, cut into 5 cm (2 in) long matchsticks

1 teaspoon aniseed seeds

a handful of fresh basil, torn

3 sprigs fresh thyme, finely chopped

sea salt and freshly ground black pepper

2 tablespoons freshly grated Pecorino Romano cheese

1 In a large frying pan heat the olive oil, add the garlic and sauté until soft but not browned.

2 Add the chilli-pepper flakes and courgette and stir well. Cover and simmer over a low heat for 10 minutes.

3 Sprinkle over the aniseed and cook for 1 minute. Remove from the heat and add the basil, thyme, salt and pepper. Toss well.

4 Transfer the courgettes to a serving dish and sprinkle with the cheese. Serve immediately.

Aniseed is digestive, and is used in the making of Sambuca, the famous Italian elderberry liqueur. The aniseed plant belongs to the same family as dill, caraway and fennel.

FAGIOLINI DI SANT'ANNA

Green Beans in Garlic Sauce

When I'm writing and run short of recipes, my friend Anna from Perugia helps me out – a saint indeed! This is one of her magic recipes: simple, straightforward and delicious.

SERVES 4

3 tablespoons olive oil

2 garlic cloves, peeled and crushed

1 large ripe tomato, skinned and chopped

550g (1 lb 4 oz) French beans, topped, tailed and halved lengthways

sea salt and freshly ground black pepper

1 Heat the oil in a medium saucepan, add the garlic and fry gently until coloured. Stir in the tomato then add the beans.

2 Add enough water to barely cover the beans, then season to taste and bring to the boil. Lower the heat, cover, and simmer for 15–20 minutes until the beans are tender.

3 Remove the lid, and increase the heat towards the end of the cooking time to reduce the juices. Serve hot or cold.

Green beans are a high-energy food, perfect for busy lifestyles.

CIPOLLE FARCITE

Baked Stuffed Onions

These stuffed onions make an ideal *contorno*, a course by themselves. Be inventive with the filling: this one I recommend, but spinach would be good too, and looks wonderful.

SERVES 4

4 medium onions, peeled
100 g (3½ oz) freshly grated
   Parmesan
85 g (3 oz) butter

3 free-range eggs
sea salt and freshly ground
   black pepper
3 tablespoons brandy

1 Cook the onions in boiling water for 15 minutes. Drain and cut in half horizontally, then scoop out two-thirds of the cores with a spoon.

2 Chop the cores and place in a bowl with the cheese, half of the butter, the eggs, and salt and pepper to taste. Mix thoroughly then spoon into the onion shells.

3 Pre-heat the oven to 200°C / 400°F / gas mark 6.

4 Melt the remaining butter in a flameproof casserole, put the onions in and then sprinkle with the brandy.

5 Bake in the pre-heated oven for 25 minutes until golden. Serve right away.

Onions, raw and cooked, contain juices that are antiseptic and good for the whole of the digestive system.

PATATE AL FORNO

Roast Potatoes with Garlic, Rosemary and Lemon

These are healthy 'roast' potatoes, made crispy and flavourful by the lemon juice: the juice caramelises slightly on the surface starch of the potatoes, and turns them golden. The dish is best made with Italian new potatoes, but you can use other varieties, old or new. I make these at the cookery school to accompany fish caught in the lake – a wonderful combination.

SERVES 4

1 kg (2 lb 4 oz) Italian new
   potatoes
125 ml (4½ fl oz) olive oil
leaves from 1 sprig fresh
   rosemary, finely chopped
juice of 2 lemons

grated zest of 1 unwaxed lemon
3 garlic cloves, peeled and
   finely chopped
sea salt and freshly ground
   black pepper

1 Pre-heat the oven to 200°C / 400°F / gas mark 6.

2 Scrub the potatoes and cut into 2½ cm (1 in) cubes. Parboil for 10 minutes and drain into a bowl.

3 In a separate bowl, prepare the dressing, using the olive oil, rosemary, lemon juice and zest and the garlic.

4 Pour this dressing over the hot potatoes and mix, then place in a roasting dish. Stirring periodically, bake for 25 minutes until golden.

5 Season with salt and pepper, and serve warm or cold.

POLPETTE DI PATATE E RICOTTA

Potato and Ricotta Cheese Balls

This Sicilian speciality is very child friendly, as they love to discover the Ricotta in the middle. Ricotta is very light and nutritious, and I always have it in my fridge, because it can be used in so many recipes, both sweet and savoury.

SERVES 4

1 kg (2 lb 4 oz) old potatoes, scrubbed
4 free-range eggs
100 g (3½ oz) freshly grated Parmesan
sea salt and freshly ground black pepper

a handful of fresh flat-leaf parsley, chopped
100 g (3½ oz) dry breadcrumbs
450 g (1 lb) Ricotta cheese
1 teaspoon freshly grated nutmeg
olive oil for deep-frying

1 Boil the potatoes in their skins, then peel and mash them in a vegetable mill. Add 2 of the eggs, the grated Parmesan, some salt and pepper, the chopped parsley and a handful of the dry breadcrumbs to thicken the mixture. Amalgamate the ingredients thoroughly.

2 In a bowl, mash the Ricotta with a fork. Season with salt and pepper and a little nutmeg. Beat the remaining eggs in a small bowl.

3 Make little nests with the potato mixture in your palms dampened with water, and fill up the hollows with a sponful of Ricotta. Seal with more of the potato mixture to form a ball.

4 Dip each ball first into the beaten egg, then the remaining breadcrumbs. Deep-fry in olive oil until golden. Drain well and serve warm.

Best eaten in spring when ricotta is at its best, creamiest and most flavoursome. The milk is at its richest because the sheep have been feeding on the lush green spring grass.

TORTA DI MELANZANA

Aubergine Cake

One of my all-time favourites: aubergine, fried in a coating of egg and Parmesan until golden and crispy, then layered with Mozzarella cheese and a fresh tomato sauce. Ideal for entertaining, it can be made in advance and re-heated at the last minute.

SERVES 4

1 medium aubergine, thinly sliced
sea salt and freshly ground black pepper
900 g (2 lb) fresh ripe tomatoes
1 onion, finely chopped
1 garlic clove, crushed
6 tablespoons olive oil
1 teaspoon sugar

1 handful of fresh basil leaves, torn
2 tablespoons strong white unbleached
   flour
4 free-range eggs
3 tablespoons freshly grated Parmesan,
   plus extra to sprinkle on top
350 g (12 oz) Mozzarella cheese, sliced

1 Sprinkle the aubergine slices with salt, place in a colander, cover and weight down. Leave for 30 minutes.

2 Put the tomatoes in a bowl, cover with boiling water for about a minute, then plunge into cold water. Peel off the skins, then chop the tomatoes.

3 In a large saucepan, heat 2 tablespoons of the olive oil, add the garlic and cook until coloured, then add the onion and cook gently until softened. Add the tomatoes and sugar, bring to the boil, then simmer for 40 minutes, uncovered, to allow the sauce to reduce. Season with salt and pepper and add a few basil leaves. The sauce should be thick and concentrated.

4 Rinse the aubergine and pat dry. Dip the slices in flour and set aside.

5 Whisk the eggs in a bowl and add the Parmesan cheese. In a frying pan, heat the remaining olive oil. Dip the aubergine in the egg mixture and fry until golden on both sides. Drain on absorbent kitchen paper and set aside.

6 Pre-heat the oven to 190°C/375°F/gas mark 5. Assemble the dish in a 20 cm (8 in) spring-release cake tin. Place a layer of the aubergines in the bottom, add a third of the cheese, tomato sauce and basil leaves. Then add further layers, finishing with a layer of aubergine slices.

7 Sprinkle over Parmesan cheese and bake in the oven for 20–25 minutes, until golden.

Mozzarella can be made from cows' milk, but the genuine cheese is made from buffalo milk. Mozzarella made in other countries is usually a poor substitute, as it is often rubbery and does not have the same melting qualities.

PATATE E ZUCCHINI AL FORNO CON AGLIO

Roast Potatoes with Courgettes, Garlic and Herbs

Spunta potatoes, which my father grows, are rich and yellow fleshed, with lots of moisture. Even the soil in which they travel – in hand-sewn sacks – smells good!

SERVES 4

6 large Italian new potatoes
 (*Spunta*), scrubbed
2 medium courgettes
6 tablespoons olive oil
3 garlic cloves, peeled and
 crushed

2 sprigs fresh rosemary,
 chopped
sea salt and freshly ground
 black pepper

1 Pre-heat the oven to 200°C / 400°F / gas mark 6.

2 Cut the potatoes and courgettes into 2.5 cm (1 in) chunks. Put the courgettes in a bowl and set aside.

3 In a 35 x 23 cm (14 x 9 in) baking dish, mix the olive oil and the garlic paste. Add the potatoes and coat well with the mixture. Bake for 30–45 minutes and baste frequently.

4 Add the courgettes and rosemary to the baking dish, and toss well, then bake for a further 10 minutes. Sprinkle with salt and pepper and serve at once.

Any potatoes will do, but Egyptian new potatoes would be the nearest to Spunta.

PATATE DELLA NONNA

Grandmother's Potatoes

This reminds me of home, and incorporates two of our firm family favourites: potatoes and spinach. The potato 'cake' can be made ahead of time and re-heated. Serve cut in wedges as a *contorno*, a separate vegetable course.

SERVES 4

450g (1 lb) Italian new potatoes (*Spunta*), peeled

sea salt and freshly ground black pepper

a handful of fresh flat-leaf parsley, finely chopped

½ teaspoon freshly grated nutmeg

100g (3½ oz) freshly grated Parmesan

2 large free-range eggs, beaten

225g (8 oz) spinach, washed well and finely chopped

55g (2 oz) unsalted butter

55g (2 oz) fresh breadcrumbs, toasted

1 Cook the potatoes well, then drain and mash. Add salt, pepper, parsley, nutmeg, Parmesan, eggs and spinach, and mix well.

2 Pre-heat the oven to 200°C / 400°F / gas mark 6.

3 Grease a 25 cm (10 in) cake tin with some of the butter, then cover the bottom with half the breadcrumbs. Spread over the potato mixture, and cover with the remaining breadcrumbs.

4 Dot with the remaining butter and bake until golden: about 10 minutes.

Italians use a lot of breadcrumbs in cooking. We tend to dry pieces of stale bread in a low oven until very brittle, then crush them with a rolling pin. Store in an airtight jar, and use when needed.

INSALATE

In my family, one of the separate courses that was regularly served, every lunchtime, was a salad. My grandmother insisted that eating an *insalata* after the main course was digestive, a healthy way to settle one's stomach. She – as do many Italians – preferred bitter greens which are called *cicoria*, a term for many varieties of wild and cultivated greens. (Dandelion leaves, for instance – perhaps even the wild ancestor of the *cicoria* family – are picked for salads. They have a bitter flavour, and are valued for their high iron content.)

I really relish the salad course in the Italian diet, and I love the simplicity of the dressing as well: often just a very good extra-virgin olive oil mixed with lemon juice (occasionally wine or balsamic vinegar) and seasoning. Even the dressing for salads can contribute to health, for olive oil is mono-unsaturated, therefore it doesn't heighten your blood cholesterol levels as other oils might. And, of course, it contains many nutrients, comes from organically grown fruit, and is produced in a non-commercial, natural way. When making olive-oil dressings, or sprinkling oil on to a dish, use an extra-virgin oil. Its taste is magnificent and it varies from region to region: lighter in the north, heavier in the south – but all are unique and exciting. Never cook with an extra-virgin oil: that would be a waste of what I call 'green gold'.

When making leaf salads, there are a few basic rules: do not buy limp lettuce or lettuce that has yellow leaves or dark brown spots, which is an indication of old age. Fresh lettuce is uniformly green and almost stands up on its own. The leaves are springy and squeaky when shaken, and the head should feel solid. The same applies to the so-called 'designer leaves', among them rocket, *radicchio* and *frisée*. Never wash any salad leaves until you are just about ready to make the salad. Drain the leaves well in a colander, then gently roll them in paper towel to absorb excess water. If the lettuce is wet the oil will not adhere to it. Dress at the last minute as well.

Of course they don't just use leaves in salads in Italy, and there are many vegetable salads, once again revealing the Italian love for vegetables of all kinds. I have included a wide selection here – among them artichokes, fennel, aubergines and potatoes – and hope you will enjoy them. It is said that a good salad should contain a root, fruit and shoot for a perfect balance of nutrients: I think you'll find that most of the following adhere to this admonition to a certain extent.

INSALATA DI MELANZANE E CIPOLLE

Aubergine, Potato and Onion Salad

This recipe came from a family friend in Calabria, Salvatore Veltri. I spent ten days, one hot summer, learning how to cook delicious red onions, which he grows for export. The Tropea onion is picked in early spring and late summer, and its bulbs are intense violet, round, oval or long. They are sweet and fleshy, and eminently suitable for salads and raw dishes.

SERVES 4

1 firm aubergine, weighing about
  200g (7 oz)
sea salt and freshly ground black pepper
200g (7 oz) Italian new potatoes
2 red onions, peeled
a handful of fresh mint leaves
a handful of fresh oregano
1–2 tablespoons white-wine vinegar
3 tablespoons extra-virgin olive oil

1 Peel, wash and boil the entire aubergine for 10 minutes in plenty of boiling water. Drain and cool. Cut it up into strips and place on a plate.

2 Peel, slice and boil the potatoes until tender. Drain and add to the aubergine.

3 Chop the onions finely, and add to the aubergine and potato, along with the herbs, vinegar and oil. Season with salt and pepper, and mix well. Serve at room temperature.

Lino Businco, teacher of general pathology at Rome University, defines onions as 'friends of the blood, keeping it as fluid and fluent as the blood of a young man'.

INSALATA DI RUCOLA E FICHI

Rocket and Fig Salad

Rocket is a member of the same family as mustard and cress, which is obvious when you bite into it and encounter its bitter, sharp and peppery flavour. It was once cultivated in Britain, but went out of fashion for centuries until very recently, when Italian imports caused a happy renaissance. Now rocket is the leaf of the moment, appearing in many of the most fashionable salads; it can also be used to make an extremely pungent pesto.

SERVES 4

225g (8 oz) rocket leaves
125g (4½ oz) fresh figs, quartered
1 tablespoon freshly squeezed
  lemon juice
2–3 tablespoons fruity extra-virgin
  olive oil
sea salt and freshly ground black pepper

1 Wash the rocket well, tear into rough pieces, and dry it thoroughly.

2 Mix the quartered figs with the leaves, and add the lemon juice, oil and seasoning. Serve at once.

INSALATA DI SICILIA

Tomato, Mint and Red Onion Salad

I have very fond memories of this salad and of eating it in Syracuse, Sicily, with my father. Some friends there grow lettuces, and this salad is what we ate – part of a wonderful meal – after a long dusty drive to their farm. It was the first time I had seen tomatoes, onion and mint together – and it is a stunning combination.

SERVES 4

4 firm, bright red tomatoes
½ small red onion, peeled and finely chopped
a handful of fresh mint, finely chopped
3 tablespoons extra-virgin olive oil
zest and juice of 1 unwaxed lemon
sea salt and freshly ground black pepper

1 Slice the tomatoes and arrange on a large plain plate.

2 Sprinkle the onion and mint over the tomatoes, and then drizzle with oil and lemon juice. Sprinkle over the finely chopped zest of the lemon, and season with salt and pepper.

3 Allow all the ingredients to come together for 20 minutes, and then serve.

All the ingredients must be of the very best quality. When tomatoes at home are not in season, do choose tomatoes that have been grown in a sunny country, so that some of the goodness of the southern sun will have sweetened the flesh, and produced a beautiful ripe tomato with a deep red skin.

BROCCOLI IN INSALATA

Broccoli Salad

The Italian love of vegetables is amply illustrated by the fact that they even eat broccoli in a salad. A crispness comes from the raw carrot, a softer texture from the cooked broccoli. The lemon juice recognisably enhances the flavour of the broccoli, just as it does many other cooked green vegetables (particularly spring greens, one of my favourite vegetables).

SERVES 4

450 g (1 lb) broccoli florets
sea salt and freshly ground black pepper
4 small carrots
juice of 4 lemons
½ teaspoon dried chilli-pepper flakes
2 tablespoons fruity olive oil

1 Cook the broccoli florets in rolling, boiling, salted water for 7 minutes. Drain and refresh under cold water to prevent further cooking. Drain again and leave to cool.

2 Scrape the carrots and shred them into thin strips.

3 Mix the carrots and cold broccoli together, and dress with lemon juice, chilli, salt, pepper and oil.

Broccoli is a type of flowering cabbage developed in Calabria, hence its alternative name of calabrese. Buy broccoli when it is bright green, not yellow. Look at the stalk end, which ought to appear as if newly cut; if it looks dry, the broccoli could be tough. Broccoli, being green, contains Vitamins A and C as well as many minerals. You could also try purple sprouting broccoli, which has a delicious, nutty flavour.

INSALATA DI RINFORZO

Cauliflower Salad

The Italian name means 'reinforced salad', because it is served at Christmas time to 'back up' or 'reinforce' the other dishes on the table, acting as a refreshing interlude between courses.

SERVES 4

1 cauliflower

sea salt and freshly ground black pepper

55g (2 oz) green olives, halved and pitted

1 tablespoon good-quality capers

1 tablespoon sun-dried tomatoes, chopped

1 roasted red pepper (*see* page 123), finely chopped

a handful of fresh flat-leaf parsley, finely chopped

2 tablespoons extra-virgin olive oil

2 tablespoons red-wine vinegar

1 Cut the cauliflower into small uniform florets. Rinse well in cold water and drain. Put the florets in a large pot and add cold water to cover. Add 1 teaspoon salt and bring to the boil. Boil the cauliflower until *al dente*, about 5–6 minutes, then drain.

2 Meanwhile, in a salad bowl, combine the olives, capers, sun-dried tomatoes, roasted pepper, parsley and seasoning. Then add the cauliflower.

3 In a small bowl, whisk together the olive oil and wine vinegar. Add to the vegetables and toss well. Cover the bowl and leave the salad to marinate in a cool place for about an hour before serving.

Cauliflowers in Italy are at their best in the winter, and feature frequently in cooking in December. Olives too will have just been harvested, and will be used for the first time at the Christmas dinner table.

INSALATA DI SPINACI E PATATE

Spinach and Potato Salad

The combination of these two ingredients is rather delicious, creating a salad that is warming and satisfying, with a meaty texture. As these two vegetables are commonly cooked together in the Indian sub-continent, perhaps Marco Polo had a hand in bringing the idea back to Europe.

SERVES 4

1 kg (2 lb 4 oz) spinach

55g (2 oz) unsalted butter

sea salt and freshly ground black pepper

3 tablespoons extra-virgin olive oil

1 dessertspoon balsamic vinegar

4 medium Italian new potatoes, scrubbed and thinly sliced

1 Wash the spinach well and remove any tough stems. Cook in a large pan, with only the water clinging to the leaves, until wilted.

2 Add the butter to the spinach along with some salt and pepper and the oil and vinegar. Mix very well to season all the spinach leaves.

3 Boil the potato slices until tender and mix into the spinach. Serve warm.

This is a good salad to serve in the winter, giving the carbohydrate of the potato and the nutrients of the green vegetable, plus lots of energy and health.

CARCIOFI CON PESTO

Artichoke Salad with Pesto

I have already given a pesto recipe, but this one is different, using less basil and garlic. This is because the artichokes have such a special flavour, and I didn't want the pungency of those two ingredients to overpower it.

SERVES 4

6 small artichokes
juice of 2 lemons

Pesto
55 g (2 oz) fresh basil leaves
3 tablespoons extra-virgin
  olive oil

1 garlic clove, peeled and
  crushed
3 tablespoons freshly grated
  Parmesan
1 tablespoon freshly grated
  Pecorino Romano cheese
2 tablespoons pine kernels

1 To prepare the artichokes, snap back the tough leaves and pull down, working your way around the layers. Stop when you get to the pale yellow, tender leaves. Cut off the tops of the remaining leaves, leaving about 2½ cm (1 in) of leaf.

2 Use a paring knife to trim away the dark green areas along the base. Trim off the base of the stem end and cut away the tough fibres around the stem end, leaving just the light-coloured, tender, centre portion. Cut the artichokes in half, lengthways. Using a paring knife, carefully cut away the fuzzy choke, trying to cut just at the point where choke and heart meet. Keep in acidulated water, ie water with the lemon juice added.

3 Boil the artichokes for 10 minutes if small, a bit longer if larger. Drain and leave to cool.

4 To make the best pesto (*see* also page 99), get a large pestle and mortar and grind all the ingrdients together slowly by hand, until a smooth paste is formed.

5 Pour the pesto over the artichokes, and serve at room temperature.

If fresh artichokes aren't available, you can use fresh artichoke hearts – or indeed hearts from a tin or jar which have been drained then marinated in extra-virgin olive oil with a little garlic.

INSALATA DI PEPERONI E CAPPERI

Pepper Salad with Capers

This salad always seemed to be available on the dresser when hunger struck in my childhood. All we needed to do for an emergency snack was cut a substantial hunk of bread and top it with the salad and its juices.

SERVES 4

3 medium yellow peppers, roasted
 (*see* page 123)
4 large ripe tomatoes
1 medium garlic clove, peeled
a handful of fresh basil leaves, torn
a handful of fresh mint leaves, torn
2 tablespoons extra-virgin olive oil
sea salt and freshly ground black pepper
2 tablespoons best-quality capers in
 balsamic vinegar

1 Allow the peppers to cool before skinning and de-seeding. Cut into thin strips.

2 Cut the tomatoes into pieces. Finely chop the garlic and mix with the tomato in a bowl. Add the basil and mint, oil, salt and pepper, and mix very well.

3 Arrange the pepper strips on a serving dish and pour the prepared tomato 'sauce' over them. Mix well, and leave to infuse for 30 minutes.

4 Serve sprinkled with the capers and some extra mint leaves if desired.

Tomatoes and basil should be grown together – companion planting – because the fragrant oils of the basil will keep aphids and other insects away from the tomatoes. Thus it seems entirely natural that they should be eaten together.

INSALATA DI FINOCCHIO E ARANCIA

Fennel and Orange Salad

This Sicilian salad is colourful and unusual, and packed full of Vitamin C. A traditional story tells that when there is nothing to eat in Sicily there are always blood oranges, so called because of their deep red colour.

SERVES 4

6 medium blood oranges (or navel oranges)
1 medium fennel bulb, trimmed and
 cut into thin strips
2 tablespoons finely minced fennel leaves
3 tablespoons finely chopped fresh walnuts
2 tablespoons fruity extra-virgin olive oil
sea salt and freshly ground black pepper
8 cos lettuce leaves

1 Peel the oranges and remove as much of the pith as possible. Slice the oranges into thin rounds and place them in a shallow dish, slightly overlapping.

2 Sprinkle over the fennel strips, fennel leaves and walnuts. Drizzle the olive oil over and sprinkle with salt and pepper.

3 Cover and let stand at room temperature for several hours. Every so often, tilt and turn the salad so that the oil and juices that have collected flow over and around the oranges.

4 To serve, arrange the salad on a bed of cos lettuce leaves, and pour the juices over.

This illustrates the sweet and sour flavours that are so prevalent in the south. The acidity comes from the blood oranges – they are more tangy than navels – and the sweetness from the fennel.

INSALATA CON ERBE

Green Salad with Wild Herbs

This recipe comes from the deeply religious south of the country, where every facet of life seems to be analysed or dissected in terms of superstition or religion. Here we use seven herbs because seven represents the number of the cardinal virtues.

SERVES 4

1 crisp fresh cos lettuce

½ Treviso radicchio

a handful of rocket leaves

a large handful in total of 7 wild herbs from the garden (ie basil, parsley, thyme, marjoram, chives, sage and mint), finely chopped together

1 fennel bulb, thinly sliced

Dressing

3 tablespoons best extra-virgin olive oil

1 tablespoon freshly squeezed lemon juice

sea salt and freshly ground black pepper

1 Wash and pat dry all the salad leaves. Wash, dry and finely chop the herbs. Mix the leaves and herbs together, and then toss in the fennel slices.

2 Mix all the dressing ingredients together, seasoning to taste with salt and pepper.

3 To preserve the crispness of the leaves, dress the salad immediately before serving.

INSALATA D'ORTO

Garden Salad

This is an invention of mine, and it came about simply through opening the fridge and seeing what was there. It's full of texture and flavour, and looks good as well.

SERVES 4

2 celery sticks

2 carrots, peeled

1 small red onion, peeled

8 small vine-ripened tomatoes

a handful of fresh flat-leaf parsley

a handful of fresh mint

3 tablespoons fruity extra-virgin olive oil

1 tablespoon lemon juice

sea salt and freshly ground black pepper

1 Roughly chop the celery, carrots and onion. Cut the tomatoes in half. Chop the parsley and mint finely.

2 Put all the ingredients in a bowl, and season to taste with salt and pepper. Mix together and serve at once.

Celery should be enjoyed when yellow, not green. The flavour is superior, more mellow, as it has had time to mature. Celery has great digestive properties, being highly alkaline. (This is why it is often served with cheese, which is acidic.)

INSALATA DELLA NONNA

Grandmother's Special Salad

This hearty salad is full of goodness. The combination of beans and potatoes also make it a filling snack.

SERVES 4

450 g (1 lb) French beans, cut into bite-sized pieces
450 g (1 lb) new potatoes, boiled
sea salt and freshly ground black pepper
1 handful of freshly chopped oregano
2 tablespoons freshly squeezed lemon juice
4 tablespoons extra virgin olive oil
1 clove garlic, finely crushed
6 tomatoes (preferably vine-ripened), roughly chopped

1 Steam the French beans for approximately 7 minutes, or until tender.

2 Cook the potatoes in boiling salted water for 10–15 minutes, or until tender, depending on their size.

3 While the beans and potatoes are cooking, mix the lemon juice and oil together with the seasonings, herbs and garlic.

4 Add the tomatoes and mix well with the potatoes and beans.

I have a huge passion for extra-virgin olive oil. It is worth experimenting with different oils – in the same way many people try wines – to find one that you particularly like. The best are dark green and strong in flavour. Remember that price is usually a good indication of quality.

PANZANELLA ALLA MINORI

Bread, Onion and Tomato Salad

There are many variations of this salad, which originates in Tuscany. It is a bread salad created, like so many other Tuscan dishes, to utilise left-over stale bread. In this context, bread mops up all the delicious juices of the vegetables, and really is a bonus – especially when you have a large number of mouths to feed.

SERVES 4

200 g (7 oz) coarse white bread, crusts removed
5 ripe tomatoes, preferably on the vine, finely chopped
1 red onion, peeled and finely chopped
½ cucumber, finely chopped
2 celery sticks, finely chopped
6 tasty black olives, pitted and chopped
a handful of fresh basil, torn
a handful of fresh mint, coarsely chopped
80 ml (3 fl oz) extra-virgin olive oil
25 ml (1 fl oz) white-wine vinegar
sea salt and freshly ground black pepper

1 Cut the bread into chunky pieces and put into a salad bowl and sprinkle with 1 tablespoon water.

2 Add all the other vegetable and herb ingredients, and toss.

3 Dress with the oil and vinegar, and season with salt and pepper. Stir well and leave for half an hour before serving.

An open-textured bread – one made with olive oil – is best, as it holds its shape and does not disintegrate. A bought ciabatta, or the olive bread on page 166, would be good.

PANE

Most cultures throughout the world have a tradition of bread-making, and it is particularly strong in Italy. No Italian meal is complete without bread, and no Italian cook worth his or her salt would ever offer food without the accompaniment of some sort of bread. Its inclusion in a meal is automatic, as much a part of laying the table as arranging the cutlery and folding the napkins.

Every day the Italians might eat a rustic, plain type of risen bread, one with an open texture, probably made with olive oil: a ciabatta, perhaps, or a *Pugliese* bread: one made with semolina and hard wheat, from Puglia in southern Italy (which lasts longer than most other Italian breads). But many breads can have other ingredients baked within them, like the cheese and olive breads in the pages following. Some breads are made rolled around a filling, and others are baked flat as well, to hold a topping. The pizza from Naples is perhaps the most familiar, but there are variations all over Italy: the focaccia or hearth bread of Genoa and elsewhere, and the *schiacciata* of Emilia-Romagna. Breads can be savoury or sweet (which are wonderful served for breakfast) and there are also many festive breads, made traditionally at times of religious significance or celebration, such as Easter and Christmas.

Italian breads go stale quite quickly, often because they are baked without the preservative action of salt. This is particularly so in Tuscany, where a heavy salt tax in the Middle Ages led to bakers devising bread recipes which did not need to use salt. As a result, there are many recipes in the Tuscan canon which utilise stale bread: bread soup, *pappa al pomodoro*; and *panzanella*, a bread salad (*see* page 159). Bread is also made into *crostini* or croûtons, *bruschetta* with its drizzled topping of olive oil (or something more ambitious), and breadcrumbs, an important ingredient in many regional cuisines.

I bake bread several times a week, and I eat it every day. It represents a significant part of my diet, as it is a complex carbohydrate, releasing energy slowly into the body. If I eat bread at a meal, to accompany a salad or vegetable dish, this healthy combination will keep me going well until the next mealtime, and I won't be tempted to have a less than healthy snack.

Something wonderful happens to your kitchen and your life when bread-making becomes a regular activity: the fragrance and suspense of it; the sharing of its warmth and goodness when it comes out of the oven; the very fact that we care enough to take the time: all these remind us that home is a fine place to be. Though perhaps a small thing, bread-making to me seems like a counterweight to the forces pulling family and friends apart. In fact, bread-making is the one culinary activity I get really passionate about, and I think it would be a wonderful thing to encourage children to participate in, allowing their sense of achievement and pride to begin.

BIGA

Italian Bread Starter

I believe this to be the cornerstone of great Italian bread. Wheat in Italy is traditionally poor for bread-making, so *bigas* were designed to boost and enhance the performance of breads, much as a turbo enhances the perfomance of a car (a simile coined by one of my students). A *biga* gives the bread those 'eyes', the wonderful open texture, and the deep delicious smell to the dough. It can be incorporated at the beginning stage of any bread: add 50 ml (2 fl oz) of the *biga* to the well in the flour when you are adding the liquid and foaming yeast.

2.5 g (⅛ oz) fresh yeast
150 ml (¼ pint) water
   (hand hot)

125 g (4½ oz) strong white
   unbleached flour

1   Crumble the yeast into the water in a bowl, add the flour and mix to form a thick batter.

2   Cover with a damp tea-towel, and leave to ferment at room temperature for between 24 and 36 hours before use, but no longer, as it will get tangier and sourer. Keep the cloth permanently damp.

Please note that you will still have to add yeast to your recipe, even if you are using a biga. *And if you find there is slight separation in the* biga, *don't be alarmed, simply stir it all back together.*

PANE DI OLIVE
Olive Bread

I found this recipe when I was on a food-tasting trip in Liguria, and of the many olive breads we tried, this was our favourite. Do use the best olives you can, preferably the ones preserved in oil, as these have far more flavour. You may have to spend quite a time pitting aromatised olives from a deli, but it will all be worth it! And once you have mastered the recipe, you could ring the changes by adding an herb: thyme or oregano would be good.

MAKES 4 SMALL LOAVES

15g (½ oz) fresh yeast
200–250 ml (7–9 fl oz) water
   (hand hot)
450g (1 lb) strong white
   unbleached flour

½ teaspoon sea salt
olive oil
150g (5½ oz) black olives,
   pitted and chopped

1 Mix the yeast and 60 ml (2 fl oz) of the water. Cover and leave to froth for about 15 minutes.

2 Put the flour and salt in a bowl together with 3 tablespoons of the olive oil. Pour the frothy yeast into the flour along with most of the remaining water, and work it into a stiff, sticky dough. Add the remaining water if necessary.

3 Knead for about 10 minutes or until the dough is smooth and elastic, adding a little more flour if necessary. Add the olives and knead them into the dough.

4 Put another tablespoon of oil into the bowl and turn the dough in it to grease the surface and prevent any crust forming. Cover the bowl with a damp cloth and leave the dough to rise in a warm place for about 1½ hours, or until doubled in bulk.

5 Knead the dough again for a few minutes, then divide into four balls. Place the balls on an oiled baking tray. Press them down gently, or shape them in any way you like. Let the dough rise again, covered, for an hour.

6 Pre-heat the oven to 240°C / 475°F / gas mark 9.

7 Brush the loaves with water to soften the crust, and bake in the pre-heated oven for about 30 minutes. Cool on a wire rack.

Olive oil is a monounsaturated fat, and olives therefore are a storehouse of this. Olives contain many minerals as well as Vitamins A and E. Green are more astringent than black, and small olives are usually more intense in flavour than larger ones. Experiment!

FOCACCIA DI LIGURIA CON FONTINA

Ligurian Bread with Potato and Fontina Cheese

Focaccia can be thick or thin, depending on the part of Italy you are in: often fashionably thin in the elegant north and fatter in the more rustic south. This particular focaccia is very thin, topped with potato slices arranged like fish scales, and the local mountain Fontina cheese. It is good, warming, winter food.

SERVES 8

7 g (¼ oz) fresh yeast

350 ml (12 fl oz) water (hand hot)

7 tablespoons *Biga* (see page 165)

3 tablespoons extra-virgin olive oil

450 g (1 lb) strong white unbleached flour

1½ teaspoons sea salt

Topping

250 g (9 oz) new potatoes, scrubbed and thinly sliced

sea salt and freshly ground blackpepper

2 garlic cloves, peeled

125 g (4½ oz) Fontina cheese, sliced, rind removed

olive oil

4 teaspoons finely chopped fresh rosemary

1 Whisk the yeast into the warm water in a large mixing bowl, and add the *biga* and olive oil. Mix the flour and salt together and stir into the yeast mixture to form a soft dough.

2 Turn the dough out of the bowl on to a floured surfce and knead for 8–10 minutes until smooth and elastic. Place in a lightly oiled bowl, cover with clingfilm, and leave to rise for 1–1½ hours, or until doubled in size.

3 Meanwhile, for the topping, blanch the potato slices in salted water for 5 minutes, then drain and dry. Keep to one side.

Turn the dough out of the bowl and press into a 28 x 43 cm (11 x 17 in) baking sheet, forming the dough into an oval shape.

4 Dimple the dough and spread with the garlic, crushed, sliced potatoes, cheese, a little olive oil and some salt and pepper. Finish by sprinkling the chopped rosemary over the top. Leave to rest for 20 minutes at room temperature.

5 Meanwhile, pre-heat the oven to 200°C/400°F/gas mark 6.

6 Bake the bread for 25–30 minutes, until the top is golden. Cool on a wire rack and eat whilst still warm.

Make sure you use good potatoes: Italian new potatoes, such as Spunta *or* Elvira, *are delicious and can be found occasionally in supermarkets. However, any waxy new potato from a hot country with a good soil can be substituted.*

167

PANE CON POMODORI E CIPOLLE ROSSE

Tomato and Red Onion Bread

This robustly flavoured loaf originated in Tropea in the southern Italian region of Calabria where tomatoes and onions flourish, and strong peppery dishes are favoured.

MAKES 1 LOAF

30 g (1 oz) fresh yeast
150 ml (¼ pint) water (hand hot)
450 g (1 lb) strong white flour
2 teaspoons sea salt
450 g (1 lb) ripe tomatoes

1 tablespoon olive oil
2 red onions, halved and finely sliced
3 teaspoons chopped fresh oregano
1 teaspoon dried chilli-pepper flakes

1 Dissolve the yeast in some of the water in a bowl. Leave for 5 minutes. Stir to dissolve. Mix the flour and salt together in a large bowl. Make a well in the centre of the flour and pour in the yeasted water.

2 Use a wooden spoon to draw enough of the flour into the yeasted water to form a thick paste. Cover the bowl with a tea-towel and leave to 'sponge' until frothy and risen: about 1 hour.

3 Skin the tomatoes by immersing them in boiling water for 1 minute. Score the skin with a knife and peel it away. Remove the cores and seeds and roughly chop the flesh. Reserve the flesh only.

4 Heat the olive oil in a pan then add the tomatoes, sliced onions, oregano and chilli. Cover the pan and cook gently for 10 minutes. Transfer the tomato mixture to a bowl and leave to cool.

5 Stir the cooled tomato mixture into the fermented sponge mix in the flour to make a soft, sticky dough. Add flour if the dough is too wet.

6 Turn the dough out on to a lightly floured work surface. Knead until silky and supple: about 10 minutes.

7 Put the dough in a lightly oiled bowl and cover with a damp tea-towel. Leave to rise until doubled in size: about 1 hour. Knock back, then chafe for 5 minutes (*see* page 181). Leave to rest for a further 10 minutes. Pre-heat the oven to 200°C/400°F/gas mark 6.

8 Shape the dough into a round loaf. Place on an oiled baking sheet, cover and leave until doubled in size: about 35 minutes. Bake in the oven for 45 minutes until golden and hollow sounding when tapped underneath. Cool on a wire rack.

This bread can be made in a ring shape as well, or indeed rolls (but bake for less time obviously). As a general rule of thumb, the more you knead, the less flavour a bread will have, but ironically, every bread does actually need to be kneaded.

CRESCIA

Cheese and Black Pepper Bread

This is an old family recipe, and I was very excited to see it in a Roman bakery recently (Volpetti in Testaccio). It is very, very tasty because the cheese is so rich and strong, and the pepper makes it very savoury. Eat it with wine and some fruit.

MAKES 1 LOAF

4 tablespoons water
  (hand hot)
15g (½oz) fresh yeast
4 tablespoons warm whole milk
3 large free-range eggs
175g (6oz) Pecorino Romano
  cheese, cubed

½ tablespoons coarsely ground
black pepper
175g (6oz) unsalted butter,
  melted and slightly cooled
450g (1lb) strong white
  unbleached flour
1 tablespoon olive oil

1 Place the water in a small bowl, sprinkle the yeast over it, and stir to dissolve. Let the yeast activate, covered, for about 10 minutes until foamy. Add the milk.

2 In a large bowl beat the eggs with a whisk until well blended, then add the yeast mixture. Stir in the cheese, pepper and melted butter, then the flour, a bit at a time, until a soft ball of dough is formed. Add more flour if the dough is sticky.

3 Turn the dough out on to a floured surface and knead until it is consistent in texture and feels silky to the touch: about 5 minutes. Let the dough rest, covered, on a floured surface for 10 minutes.

4 Pour the olive oil into a large bowl, place the dough in the bowl and turn to grease it. Cover the bowl with a tea-towel and leave the dough to rise until doubled in size: about 1½ hours.

5 Punch the dough down, place on a lightly floured work surface, and knead into a smooth ball. Place the bread on a greased baking sheet, and allow to rise for 30 minutes.

6 Meanwhile, pre-heat the oven to 200°C/400°F/gas mark 6.

7 Bake the bread for 30–35 minutes or until nicely browned. Cool on a wire rack.

This bread can be made in a ring shape as well, or indeed rolls (but bake for less time obviously). As a general rule of thumb, the more you knead, the less flavour a bread will have, but ironically, every bread does actually need to be kneaded.

172

CALZONE DI PREZZEMOLO

Folded Parsley Pizza

The literal translation of calzone is 'trouser leg', referring to the double thickness of fabric or, in this case, bread dough. The recipe comes from the Bar Mundial in Cassibile, Sicily, so thank you, Gianni Fronterrè. It is lighter than you might expect, not as doughy as many other calzoni, and the filling, despite being incredibly simple, is quite delicious.

MAKES 1 LARGE CALZONE

7g (¼ oz) fresh yeast
a little caster sugar
225–250 ml (8–9 fl oz) water (hand hot)
550g (1 lb 4 oz) strong white unbleached flour
15g (½ oz) salt
80–125 ml (3–4 fl oz) olive oil

1 onion, peeled and finely chopped
a very large handful of fresh flat-leaf parsley, chopped
freshly ground black pepper
350g (12 oz) Mozzarella cheese, cut into small cubes
plain flour for dusting

1 Cream the yeast with the sugar and a little of the water.

2 Mix the flour and salt in a large bowl. Add half the oil and the creamed yeast together with the remaining water. Mix with a wooden spoon to form a dough.

3 Turn out of the bowl and knead vigorously for 10 minutes until soft and pliable. Return the soft dough to a clean bowl. Cover and allow to rise until doubled in size: about 1 hour.

4 Meanwhile, prepare the filling by heating the remaining olive oil in a frying pan. Fry the onion until soft, then add the parsley and stir for 2 minutes over a medium heat. Season with pepper and leave to one side. When cool, mix in the cheese.

5 Pre-heat the oven to 200°C/400°F/gas mark 6.

6 Knock back the dough and knead for 4 minutes. Roll out into a large rectangle 38 x 20 cm (15 x 8 in). Spread the onion and cheese mixture over the dough, leaving a 1 cm (½ in) margin all round.

7 Now fold the dough lengthways into three, enclosing the filling, and place on a greased tray. Leave for 10 minutes to rise again and then dust with extra plain flour.

8 Bake in the pre-heated oven for 20 minutes until light and golden. Cool on a wire rack and then cut into thick or thin slices, for snacks or canapés. Good hot, cold or warm!

You can change the fillings, using other cheeses, or even meats. Try to use flat-leaf parsley, though, which is more intense in flavour than curly.

FOCACCIA ALL'OLIO E SALVIA

Sage and Olive Oil Bread

It's difficult to have too much of this bread, which is made with water, wine and olive oil, and has a delicate taste and light, porous texture. It is made by the sponge method, which is a quicker version of *biga*, when where you want to have flavour and texture in a shorter time. The use of the wine may be unusual, but it acts as an extra ferment, and adds a deeper flavour. The sage crisps on the top in the oven, and looks and tastes marvellous.

SERVES 4

Sponge
20 g (¾ oz) fresh yeast
125 ml (4½ fl oz) water (hand hot)
150 g (5½ oz) strong white unbleached flour

Dough
80 ml (3 fl oz) dry white wine
80 ml (3 fl oz) light olive oil
20 fresh sage leaves, chopped
15 g (½ oz) fresh yeast
350 g (12 oz) unbleached strong white flour
2 teaspoons sea salt

Topping
2 tablespoons good-flavoured olive oil
1–2 teaspoons sea salt
4 fresh sage leaves, chopped

1 To make the sponge, sprinkle the yeast over the warm water in a large mixing bowl, whisk it in and let it stand until creamy: about 10 minutes. Stir in the flour and beat until smooth. Cover tightly with clingfilm and leave it to rise until puffy and bubbling: about 30 minutes.

2 To make the dough, add the wine, olive oil, sage and yeast to the sponge mixture, then whisk in the flour and salt, just a little at a time, until the dough is very soft and sticky. Knead on a lightly floured surface, adding more flour if necessary. It should be soft but not wet.

3 Place the dough in a lightly oiled container, cover tightly, and let rise for 20 minutes.

4 Knock the dough back, and roll out to a circle about 5 mm (¼ in) thick. Place on an oiled baking sheet, cover and leave to rise for an hour.

5 At least 30 minutes before you plan to bake, pre-heat the oven to 200°C/400°F/ gas mark 6. Put a baking stone inside the oven if you have one.

6 Dimple the top of the bread. Drizzle over the oil and sprinkle with salt and sage.

7 Place the bread in the well pre-heated oven (on the baking stone if appropriate). Spray the oven with cold water from a spritzer 3 times during the first 10 minutes of cooking. Bake for 25–30 minutes altogether until golden brown. Remove from the oven and cool.

This is a great bread to conquer: once you have the hang of it, you can experiment in many different ways, changing the herbs inside and on top, for instance. You could use dried yeast instead of fresh: as a general rule, halve the quantity of fresh, as the dried is concentrated. It too needs to be activated in hand-hot water. Some breads can use easy-blend yeast, which is activated in the flour when the liquid is added.

PANE CON I FICHI

Fig Bread

This is the breakfast bread I make at the cookery school, and it is very popular. We call it *panmarino*, the Italian equivalent of *brioche*. It's light, has a very yellow interior, is rich in flavour, and keeps well. It can be made into buns; bake these for 20 minutes only.

MAKES 2 LOAVES

350g (12 oz) dried figs

grated zest and juice of
   6 unwaxed oranges

15g (½ oz) fresh yeast

150 ml (¼ pint) water
   (hand hot)

200g (7 oz) unsalted butter

450g (1 lb) strong white
   unbleached flour

1½ teaspoons sea salt

55g (2 oz) whole almonds,
   toasted

2 free-range eggs, beaten

icing sugar for dusting

1 Soak the figs in the orange juice and zest overnight. Don't worry if there is not enough juice to cover them, as long as they are moistened.

2 Dissolve the yeast in some of the water, and leave to activate for about 10 minutes. In a large bowl, rub the butter into the flour, with the salt.

3 Cut up the figs to the size of a thumbnail, and chop the almonds roughly. Add both to the flour, along with the orange zest and any leftover juice.

4 Add the yeast mixture, the beaten eggs and the remaining water. Mix first with a wooden spoon until a soft and pliable dough forms. Knead on a flat surface for 10 minutes until soft and springy. Return to a clean bowl and cover with a damp tea-towel for 3 hours. (The richer the mixture, the slower the rise.)

5 Knock back the dough and form into two rounds. 'Chafe' each round (*see* page 181) for a few minutes, then set on a baking sheet, covered, to prove for an hour.

6 Pre-heat the oven to 200°C / 400°F / gas mark 6.

7 Bake the loaves for 35 minutes until they are golden and sound hollow when you tap the base. Cool on a wire rack and dust with icing sugar.

Figs are very high in iron, potassium, calcium and zinc, and are also laxative in action because of their high fibre content. You could use fresh figs as well. This is what we do at the school as we have so many fig trees there. But try different fillings: a mixture of walnuts and seedless black grapes is good.

SCHIACCIATA DOLCE

Sweet Flatbread

In the tombs of the Etruscans, early inhabitants of Italy, there are curious drawings of daily activities, including depictions of pasta-making and bread-making. One such ancient bread was *schiacciata*, a flat bread that today has many different versions, depending on where you are in Italy. *Schiacciata* means 'squashed' or 'flattened', and in Siena it is a flat Easter cake with icing sugar on top; in Florence, an hour's drive away, it is a flat pizza with herbs and onions. This recipe, a much older version of *schiacciata*, is made with a batter-like dough and baked in a deepish rectangular baking tray.

MAKES 1 LARGE LOAF

175 ml (6 fl oz) water (hand hot), plus
  2 tablespoons

15 g (½ oz) fresh yeast

275 g (10 oz) strong white unbleached
  flour

1 teaspoon olive oil

1 large free-range egg, lightly beaten

150 g (5½ oz) unsalted butter, melted

40 g (1½ oz) caster sugar

1 tablespoon each of grated unwaxed
  orange and lemon zests

⅛ teaspoon powdered saffron

1 tablespoon vanilla extract

icing sugar for dusting

1   Pour all the water into a bowl. Add the yeast and stir to dissolve, then leave for 5 minutes to froth.

2   Gradually add the measured flour and mix with your hands until a ball of dough is formed. Knead the dough vigorously on a lightly floured surface.

3   Oil a bowl, add the dough and turn the dough in the oil to coat it. Cover the bowl and leave the dough to rise until doubled in size: about 1 hour.

4   Punch the dough down in the bowl, then add the egg and all but 2 tablespoons of the melted butter, the sugar, zests, saffron and vanilla. Use a wooden spoon and gently incorporate the ingredients. The dough will be very soft and sticky. Add more flour if necessary. Mix for 10 minutes.

5   Use half the remaining melted butter to grease a baking sheet with a lip, measuring 30 x 25 cm (12 x 10 in). Using a spatula, pour the dough on the sheet and smooth it out to the edges. Brush the remaining melted butter over the top. Let the dough rise in a warm place, covered, for about 1½ hours.

6   Pre-heat the oven to 200° C / 400° F / gas mark 6.

7   Bake the bread for 20–25 minutes until nicely golden on top. Cool on a wire rack. Cut into squares and dust with icing sugar.

The bread has a slightly sweet flavour, and is perfect warm for breakfast, or for tea. It keeps well, for up to two days.

179

COPPIA FERRARESE
Enriched Bread Rolls

Ferrara is famous for its water, which is why the bread of this region is so good. The recipe came from talking to a baker in the piazza one evening, who was insistent that this was the one and only recipe (there are many imitations). As few of us have access to Ferrara water, bottled still Italian water will do!

MAKES ABOUT 12 ROLLS

7 g (¼ oz) fresh yeast
200 ml (7 fl oz) water
   (hand hot)
500 g (18 oz) strong white
   unbleached flour

2 teaspoons sea salt
3 tablespoons *Biga* (*see* page 165)
3 tablespoons olive oil
3 tablespoons semolina for
   sprinkling

1 Dissolve the yeast in some of the hand hot water.

2 Mix the flour and salt together. Make a well in the flour, add the *biga*, oil, yeast mixture and most of the remaining water, and combine well together to form a soft, pliable dough.

3 Turn out on to a floured surface and knead for 8 minutes to develop the gluten. Put the dough into a clean bowl, cover with a damp cloth and leave to double in size for 1½ hours.

4 Knock back the dough and 'chafe' for 6 minutes (*see* below).

5 Cut the dough into 12 pieces, and divide each piece of dough into two strips no longer than 13 cm (5 in) in length. Twist two together like a corkscrew to join them in the middle. Do the same with the remaining strips to make 12 cross-shaped rolls. Place on a semolina-lined baking tray, and allow to prove for 20 minutes.

6 Pre-heat the oven to 200° C / 400° F / gas mark 6.

7 Fill a roasting tin with ice cubes, and place on the floor of the oven; this will create valuable moisture for the rolls and help to give them a greater colour and crust. Bake the rolls for 15–20 minutes until golden. Cool on a wire rack, and enjoy.

To 'chafe', apply a light downwards pressure to the sides of the round ball of dough, while simultaneously rotating the dough continuously in a steady clockwise motion. This lightens the bread, giving it more bubbles.

COLOMBA PASQUALE

Easter Dove Bread

Easter is a time of great celebration and holiday in Italy, much more so than Christmas. This bread – made in the shape of the dove of peace – is rich with ingredients that would have been denied in the weeks of Lent leading up to Easter. It is eaten at breakfast time, and is never cut, but broken into pieces and enjoyed with an espresso.

MAKES 2 'DOVES'

Sponge

175 ml (6 fl oz) milk

20 g (¾ oz) fresh yeast

100 g (3½ oz) strong white unbleached flour

Dough

3 large free-range eggs

1 large free-range egg yolk

100 g (3½ oz) caster sugar

100 g (3½ oz) unsalted butter

½ teaspoon sea salt

1 teaspoon vanilla extract

1 teaspoon grated unwaxed orange zest

300 g (11 oz) strong white unbleached flour

85 g (3 oz) dark or golden raisins, plus a few extra

85 g (3 oz) mixed candied fruit

To finish

100 g (3½ oz) split blanched almonds

icing sugar for dusting

1 To make the sponge, heat the milk gently until lukewarm then remove from the heat and whisk in the yeast. Stir in the flour, then cover with clingfilm and leave to rest for 30 minutes.

2 To make the dough, whisk the eggs and egg yolk with the sugar. Melt the butter and, when cool, whisk it in. Stir in the salt, vanilla and zest, then add the flour.

3 Either by hand or by machine, beat the sponge into the flour mixture until it is smooth: about 2 minutes. Then add the raisins and candied fruit. Place the dough in a buttered bowl, cover with clingfilm and leave until doubled in size: about 2 hours.

4 Punch the dough down and turn out on to a lightly floured surface. Divide into four equal pieces and shape each piece into a torpedo shape. Place one piece above another piece at right-angles, at the centre, to get a 'dove' shape, with body and outstretched wings. Do the same with the remaining pieces to make two doves. Use the extra raisins for the eyes.

5 Place each dove on a separate baking tray lined with baking parchment. Cover loosely and leave to rise again at room temperature until doubled in size: about 1 hour.

6 Pre-heat the oven to 190°C/375°F/ gas mark 5.

7 Stud the dough shapes with the almonds to look like feathers – I usually do this at the wing tips – and bake in the pre-heated oven for about 20 minutes until golden brown in colour and firm to the touch. Cool on a wire rack, and then dust with icing sugar.

The same recipe can be used to make the famous Italian Christmas bread, panettone.

PANE AL MIELE

Honey Bread

Miele, honey, has featured in cooking since the times of the Ancients. The Egyptians, Greeks and Romans all used it, not only as a sweetener, but also as a preservative. Apicius, the knowledgeable Roman gourmet, tells us that vegetables, herbs and fruit were preserved by covering them with a combination of honey and vinegar. Honey was also used in bread recipes and what were called 'honey cakes', not so much for the sweetness it offered, but because it kept the bread fresh for longer. And indeed this bread does keep quite well.

MAKES 1 LOAF

125 ml (4 fl oz) water (hand hot)

15 g (½ oz) fresh yeast

250 ml (9 fl oz) warm whole milk

175 ml (6 fl oz) clear honey, plus
   3 tablespoons

2 tablespoons melted unsalted
   butter, cooled

2 tablespoons extra-virgin olive oil

1 large free-range egg

1 tablespoon sea salt

2 tablespoons aniseed seeds

1 tablespoon of grated zest of unwaxed lemon

450 g (1 lb) strong white unbleached flour

55 g (2 oz) raisins

55 g (2 oz) shelled walnuts

55 g (2 oz) prunes, pitted and chopped

1 Place the water in a large bowl, sprinkle on the yeast, and mix to dissolve. Let the mixture sit for 10 minutes, until foamy.

2 Add the milk, the 175 ml (6 fl oz) honey, the butter, oil, egg, salt, aniseed and lemon zest to the yeast, and stir the ingredients well.

3 Add the flour and mix with your hands to obtain a ball of dough. Add additional flour (if necessary) until you have a non-stick ball. Knead well for 10 minutes to form a soft, elastic and smooth dough. Cover in a bowl and let rise for 1½ hours or until doubled in size.

4 In a small bowl mix the raisins, walnuts and prunes.

5 Punch the dough back and turn it out on to a floured surface. Knead for 2–3 minutes, then roll out into a 40 cm (16 in) circle. With a brush spread 2 tablespoons of the remaining honey over the dough and sprinkle with three-quarters of the fruit and nut filling.

6 Roll the dough up to obtain a 40 cm (16 in) long loaf, 7.5 cm (3 in) thick. Seal the ends, or the honey will seep out. Place the roll on a lightly greased baking sheet and set aside, covered, for 30 minutes to rise.

7 Pre-heat the oven to 200° C/400° F/gas mark 6.

8 Bake the bread for 30 minutes until golden. Remove to a wire rack, and with a brush spread on the remaining tablespoon of honey and then sprinkle the nut/fruit mixture over the loaf. Cool completely before eating.

Do experiment with different types of honey. I love chestnut honey and thyme honey. Indulge in some local honey if you suffer from allergies or have a reaction to pollen when abroad, as this will help lessen the symptoms.

PANE DI SPINACI DELLA NONNA

Grandmother's Spinach Bread

The Italians eat lots of bread and are crazy about greens – and this recipe combines them both. It's the sort of thing they might eat at harvest time, as an all-in-one meal (the Italian equivalent of a pasty or pie). It would be a good bread to take on a picnic. It also keeps very well.

MAKES 1 LOAF

15 g (½ oz) fresh yeast
500 ml (18 fl oz) water (hand hot)
350 g (12 oz) strong white
   unbleached flour
200 g (7 oz) fine semolina
2 teaspoons sea salt
450 g (1 lb) fresh spinach
2 tablespoons extra-virgin olive oil

1 garlic clove, peeled and minced
2 tablespoons black olives, pitted
   and finely chopped
freshly ground black pepper
1 large free-range egg white,
   beaten with 2 teaspoons water
   (egg wash)
a handful of sesame seeds

1 In a large bowl dissolve the yeast in a quarter of the water. Let it sit, covered, for 10 minutes until foamy.

2 Add the remaining water and stir well. Mix in the flour and semolina, tablespoon by tablespoon, along with the salt. Mix with your hands until a ball of dough is formed.

3 Knead vigorously for 10 minutes, then place in a lightly oiled bowl. Leave for 1½ hours, covered, until doubled in size.

4 Meanwhile prepare the filling. Wash and drain the spinach thoroughly, discarding any really tough stems. Put the leaves into a pan without any additional water, cover, and cook over a medium heat until wilted. Drain the spinach and allow it to cool. Squeeze it as dry as possible, and then chop really finely.

5 In a frying pan, heat the olive oil, add the garlic, and sauté until soft. Add the chopped spinach and cook for 2–3 minutes, then add the olives and some pepper. Remove from the heat and leave to cool completely.

6 When the dough has risen, punch it down and roll into a circle about 40 cm (16 in) in diameter. Lift the dough on to a greased baking sheet. Spoon on the spinach filling, and spread it to within 2½ cm (1 in) of the edges.

7 Roll the dough up tightly like a Swiss roll. Turn the ends under to seal. Make random 1 cm (½ in) deep slits on the top with a knife. Brush the top of the dough with egg wash and sprinkle over the sesame seeds. Cover and let the bread rise for 30 minutes.

8 Meanwhile pre-heat the oven to 200° C / 400° F / gas mark 6.

9 Bake the bread for 35 minutes until golden, then remove to a wire rack. Cool well before serving. Slice on the diagonal to reveal the wonderful swirl of the filling.

Please feel free to change the ingredients in the middle. The spinach is traditional to Naples and its environs, but you could use cheese or cooked vegetables, or a mixture.

TORTA AL TESTO

Bread of the Tile

The flat crusty appearance of this age-old peasant bread inspired its name, *testo*, which means tile in Italian. Torta al Testo is found exclusively in its native Umbria and usually *a casa*: in the home.

MAKES 8 ROUNDS

315 ml (10½ oz) water
(hand hot)
15 g (½ oz) fresh yeast
500 g (18 oz) strong white flour
1½ teaspoons salt
1 tablespoon olive oil

Filling

250 g (9 oz) Fontina cheese
125 g (4½ oz) rocket
sea salt and freshly ground
black pepper

1 Dissolve the yeast in some of the water. Leave for 5 minutes, then stir to dissolve. Mix the flour and salt together in a large bowl. Make a well in the centre and add the yeasted water and the oil. Mix in the flour and stir in the reserved water as needed to form a firm, moist dough.

2 Turn the dough out on to a lightly floured surface and knead until smooth, shiny and elastic: about 10 minutes.

3 Put the dough in a clean bowl and cover with a tea-towel. Leave to rise until doubled in size: about 30 minutes. Knock back, then leave to rest for 10 minutes.

4 Divide the dough into eight pieces. On a lightly floured surface, roll out each piece of dough to form a round 20 cm (8 in) across and 5 mm (¼ in) thick. If the dough resists rolling out, leave to rest for 1–2 minutes, then continue.

5 Heat a heavy frying pan or griddle over a medium/low heat until very hot: about 10 minutes.

6 Place one of the dough rounds in a hot pan and prick all over with a fork to prevent air bubbles. Cook until golden on both sides, flipping it over frequently to avoid schorching and to aid even cooking. Repeat with the remaining dough rounds.

7 Stack the rounds on top of each other and cover with a tea-towel to keep soft. When cool, use a sharp knife to cut around the edge of each bread, and separate it into two halves. Top one half with fontina and rocket and season with salt and pepper.

8 Place the other half on top of the filling and place the stuffed breads on two baking sheets. Bake in an oven pre-heated to 200° C / 400° F / gas mark 6, until hot and the cheese has melted. Cut into wedges and serve warm.

SCHIACCIATA DI UVA

Fresh Grape Flatbread

This sweet flat bread is best served warm as an accompaniment to coffee or as a dessert. Schiacciata means 'squashed'. Here it refers to the grapes that are squashed on the top of the dish. This delicious recipe is made to celebrate the grape harvest in Italy, which takes place in October. You can also use white grapes rather than black for variety.

MAKES 1 LARGE LOAF

Starter

15 g (½ oz) fresh yeast, or ½ teaspoons dried

150 ml (¼ pint) water (hand hot)

125 g (4½ oz) strong white flour

Dough

3 tablespoons caster sugar

15 g (½ oz) fresh yeast

175 ml (6 fl oz) water

375 g (13 oz) strong white flour

1½ teaspoons sea salt

3 tablespoons extra-virgin olive oil

Filling and topping

200 g (7 oz) raisins

1 glass *vin santo* or sweet white wine

450 g (1 lb) seedless black grapes

3 tablespoons demerara sugar

1 handful fennel seeds for
   scattering on top

1. To make the starter, sprinkle the yeast into the water. Stir to dissolve and leave for 5 minutes.

2. Add the flour and mix to form a thick batter. Cover with a tea-towel and leave to ferment at room temperature for between 12 and 36 hours, until it forms a loose, bubbling batter.

3. To make the dough, sprinkle the yeast into 100 ml (3½ fl oz) of water and stir to dissolve.

4. Mix the flour and sea salt together in a large bowl and add the sugar. Make a well in the centre of the flour and pour in the yeasted water, olive oil and the starter. Mix in the flour and stir in the remaining water to form a soft, sticky dough. Add extra water one tablespoon at a time, as necessary.

5. Turn out on a lightly floured work surface and knead the dough for about 10 minutes until smooth, silky and elastic in texture.

6. Put the dough in a lightly oiled bowl and cover with a tea-towel. Leave to rise for 1½–2 hours until doubled in size. Knock back and 'chafe' for 5 minutes, then leave to rest for about 10 minutes.

7. Divide the dough into two equal pieces. Roll out both pieces on a lightly floured work surface to form two rounds of about 24 cm (9½ in) diameter. Place one of the rounds on baking sheet that has been lightly oiled.

8. To make the filling, marinate the raisins in the wine for at least 2 hours or preferably overnight. Drain thoroughly and reserve the wine as a special treat for the baker! Spread the raisins evenly over one round of dough. Put the second round of dough on top and pinch the edges together.

9. Cover with a tea-towel and prove until doubled in size. This takes about 30 minutes. Pre-heat the oven to 200°C/400°F/gas mark 6.

10. Sprinkle with demerara sugar and fennel seeds. Bake in the pre-heated oven for approximately 45 minutes, until the crust is golden. Cool on a wire rack.

FRUTTA E NOCI

In my family, and the families of most Italians, we eat seasonal fruit fresh from the tree or vine, usually at the end of a meal. This healthy practice is completely understandable, because Italian fruit is so good, its natural sweetness intensified by the long growing season with sunny days, and by rich soil and generations of farmers who truly understand the land. Most fruits contain a good proportion of vitamins and minerals, principally Vitamins C, E and A (the latter in yellow and orange fruits).

After a winter spent eating apples, pears and a selection of preserved fruit – for fruit is traditionally dried and bottled as well – it is wonderful to look forward to the first fresh cherries, to be followed later by luscious sun-ripened peaches, apricots and figs. In my travels the length and breadth of Italy, fruit forms one of the most striking features of the landscape: the groves of lemon and orange trees, for instance, the fruit shining like beacons amongst the intensely green leaves. Fruit is bought daily at the markets, if it is not grown in the garden at home, and it is also eaten daily. I have very fond memories of my grandfather sitting at the head of the table peeling fruit for me and my sisters, and feeding it to us as if we were baby birds.

Nuts, too, play a vital role in the Italian diet. They are a storehouse of energy in the form of protein and fat, and are high in nutrients, primarily Vitamins A, B, C, D and E, and the minerals calcium and magnesium. They are eaten and enjoyed fresh, mainly in the winter months, but they are used in various forms throughout the year, in myriad recipes. Nature has actually designed them to last a year, from one harvest to the next, but once out of their shells, they start to deteriorate and oxidate, with their oils turning rancid. Any nuts, particularly those out of their shells, should be kept cool and away from strong sunlight; they should be bought from a reliable source, and used as quickly as possible.

In Italy, the harvesting of fruit and nuts calls for many festivals. In Sicily, people celebrate the flowering of almond trees in February; elsewhere, the first cherries are formally welcomed in June; and the autumn heralds the chestnut season in the north of the country, when nuts are roasted in the embers of huge bonfires. There are a multitude of recipes from every region to mark and show appreciation for the quality and quantity of fruit or nuts available locally, and I have gathered together an interesting selection. All of the recipes in this chapter are sweet, although nuts in particular are used in many savoury recipes as well. (Think of pine kernels in pesto, chestnuts in vegetable bakes and walnuts in pasta sauces.) Many of the recipes given here are for little biscuits, *biscotti*, or pastries, which in Italy are eaten not as a dessert after lunch or dinner, but as a delicious addition to coffee in the morning or afternoon.

FICHI SECCHI IN VINO

Dried Figs in Wine

One of the best fruit desserts is simply a bowl of fresh figs. I only see them in the market occasionally outside Italy, and when I do I serve them at the end of a meal with a dollop of sweet creamy mascarpone on the side. When fresh figs are not available, this is a wonderful family recipe that utilises dried figs.

SERVES 4

1 teaspoon butter
12 large dried figs
100 g (3½ oz) freshly shelled
   walnuts, chopped
125 ml (4½ fl oz) dry red wine

4 tablespoons fragrant clear
   honey
1 tablespoon grated zest of
   unwaxed orange

1   Pre-heat the oven to 180°C / 350°F/gas mark 4. Lightly grease a deep 15 cm (6 in) round casserole dish with the butter.

2   With your fingers, open each fig at the stem end to form a small hole. Stuff some of the walnut into each fig, and then place, filled side up, in a single layer in the buttered casserole.

3   In a small pot, heat the wine and honey together, stirring until the honey dissolves. Pour the mixture over the figs. Sprinkle on the zest, cover the casserole tightly with a lid, or foil, and bake in the pre-heated oven for 30 minutes.

4   Let the figs cool to room temperature in the casserole. To serve, place 3 figs on each plate and pour over some of the wine sauce. Serve with Mascarpone, if liked.

Try to buy dried figs from health-food shops which will be labelled 'preservative-free'. Many dried fruits are coated with E 220, sulphur dioxide, which may preserve and soften the fruits, but can provoke allergic reactions. When buying fresh figs, check that they are ripe. Smell each one: it should be very, very sweet and honey fragrant. Then give it a gentle squeeze: it should just give to your fingertips. The colour will depend on the variety.

TORRONE DI SESAMO

Sesame Nougat

Torrone is enjoyed throughout Italy at all times of the year, but features particularly at festive occasions such as Christmas, New Year and *Carnevale*.

MAKES ABOUT 12 SMALL SQUARES

200 g (7 oz) fragrant clear honey

55 g (2 oz) caster sugar

225 g (8 oz) sesame seeds

200 g (7 oz) whole almonds, roasted and chopped

2 teaspoons almond or sunflower oil

1 Melt the honey gently, add the sugar, and slowly bring to the boil. Add the sesame seeds and almonds, and keep stirring over a low heat until the mixture thickens.

2 Pour on to an oiled baking sheet and flatten with an oiled rolling pin. Leave to cool a little.

3 Cut into small squares with a sharp knife, then leave to cool completely. Store in an airtight tin.

Sesame seeds contain about 50 per cent of a highly unsaturated oil, and 20–25 per cent protein. They are also rich in the B vitamins, calcium, phosphorus and iron. The seeds grow in a pod which pops open as it dries: hence the expression 'Open sesame'?

TORRONCINI

Nougat

Many different varieties of nougat are made throughout Italy. This one comes from Sicily and, once again, reveals the Arabic influence. Nougat is eaten as a *merenda*, a snack, at eleven in the morning, or four in the afternoon.

MAKES 18 LITTLE SQUARES

500 g (18 oz) granulated sugar

55 g (2 oz) fragrant clear honey

250 g (9 oz) almonds, toasted and chopped

250 g (9 oz) shelled pistachio nuts, chopped

a little vegetable oil

1 Dissolve the sugar with the honey in a saucepan, then add the almonds and pistachios. Cook for 5–10 minutes over a slow heat to allow the flavours to blend.

2 Pour on to a slab of oiled marble (or a cold heatproof surface), spread out with a spatula to 5 mm (¼ in) thick, and cut immediately into long strips and then into short lengths the size of a large postage stamp.

3 When the nougat is cold, wrap each piece in waxed paper, and store in an airtight tin.

The fresher the nuts, the crunchier and more nutritious the torroncini will be. Pistachio nuts have a unique flavour, and contain about 18 per cent protein and 55 per cent unsaturated oil. Both types of nuts are great energy boosters.

MINNI DI SANTA AGATA

Baked Sweet Pastries

These dome-shaped pastries are made from a sweet pasta dough. Their shape has inspired the name which, literally translated, means 'breasts of Saint Agatha'.

MAKES ABOUT 12

Pastry

225 g (8 oz) plain white flour
  or Italian 00 plain flour
65 g (2½ oz) caster sugar
100 g (3½ oz) unsalted butter,
  cut into pieces
1 free-range egg
1 tablespoon finely grated zest
  of unwaxed lemon
a pinch of sea salt
icing sugar and cocoa powder
  for dusting

Filling

1 tablespoon shelled hazelnuts,
  toasted
1 tablespoon candied orange
  peel or mixed peel
25 g (1 oz) plain chocolate,
  50 per cent cocoa solids
225 g (8 oz) Ricotta cheese
55 g (2 oz) caster sugar
1½ teaspoons vanilla extract
1 free-range egg yolk

1 To make the pastry, put the flour and sugar into a food processor and, working on full speed, add the butter pieces gradually until well mixed. With the food processor still running, add the egg, lemon zest and salt. Turn the dough on to greaseproof paper, flatten, cover and chill in the fridge for 30 minutes. Allow to come back to room temperature before rolling.

2 For the filling, finely chop the hazelnuts and orange peel, and grate the chocolate. Push the Ricotta through a sieve into a bowl. Stir in the sugar, vanilla extract, egg yolk, peel, hazelnuts and chocolate until well mixed.

3 Pre-heat the oven to 180°C/350°F/ gas mark 4. Grease a large baking tray.

4 Roll out the pastry until about 5 mm (¼ in) thick. Cut into circles with a 3 cm (1¼ in) cutter. Put 2 teaspoons of mixture on a pastry circle and top with another pastry circle. Press to seal all round. Place on the baking tray and prick the top of each with the tines of a fork.

5 Bake the small parcels in the pre-heated oven for 20 minutes until golden. Leave to cool, then dredge with icing sugar and cocoa powder.

During a recent teaching trip in Italy, representatives of a major supermarket chain, who were attending, became very excited by this recipe, feeling it could be marketed as an Italian version of our Christmas mince pie. It certainly has as much diversity in its flavour and, in fact, tastes divine!

TORTA DI NOCE

Walnut Tart

Best served with a small glass of *Vin Santo*, perfect in the morning for breakfast (if you like a little alcohol then, as many Italians do), or for *merenda*, a little coffee break. The pastry is foolproof, wonderfully easy to handle, and it can be used in many other recipes.

SERVES 4–6

225 g (8 oz) butter
350 g (12 oz) Italian 00 plain flour
225 g (8 oz) caster sugar
4 large free-range egg yolks

225 g (8 oz) fresh walnut halves
175 g (6 oz) apricot conserve
  icing sugar for dusting

1 To make the pastry, rub the butter into the flour until the mixture is the consistency of breadcrumbs. Stir in the sugar, then add the egg yolks, and mix with your hands to form a moist, crumbly dough. Wrap in clingfilm and refrigerate for 1 hour.

2 Allow the dough a further hour to readjust to room temperature before rolling it out. During this hour, pre-heat the oven to 190°C/375°F/ gas mark 5.

3 Roast the walnut halves on a baking tray in the pre-heated oven for 7 minutes, or until only just golden. When cool, roughly chop them.

4 Divide the dough in two. Place half the dough between two sheets of floured clingfilm, and shape it into a square: use the tips of your fingers to do this, and quick, light movements. Shape the second half of the dough to the same size in the same way.

Slip one dough square on to an oblong baking tray (about 40 x 30 cm/ 16 x 12 in), using the clingfilm to help you. Remove the clingfilm.

5 Spread a thick layer of apricot conserve right to the edges of this square, then sprinkle half of the walnuts all over the top. Cover this layer with the second sheet of dough. Do not seal.

6 Bake in the middle of the pre-heated oven for 30 minutes or until the top is golden brown.

7 Remove from the oven and reduce the temperature to 170°C/325°F/ gas mark 3. Push the remaining walnut pieces evenly on to and over the still-soft pastry top. Put the tart back into the oven for a further 10 minutes.

8 Cut into small squares and leave to cool. Serve cold, dredged with icing sugar.

You could ring the changes and use different nuts: hazelnuts and almonds work well together. This is a very classical dish, from Minori, my village: you go into the local pasticceria, *buy a small square in a paper napkin, and enjoy it standing at the bar with a rich espresso. The sweetness of the tart perfectly balances the bitterness of the coffee.*

PAN ROZZO

Spiced Almond and Chocolate Cake

This is dedicated to almond and chocolate lovers. It is a speciality of the Abruzzi e Molise, an area on the east coast of Italy, which produces magnificent almonds. Very little is known of this region in the culinary sense, apart from its almonds.

SERVES 6

55 g (2 oz) Italian 00 plain flour
55 g (2 oz) potato flour
a pinch of powdered cinnamon
4 free-range eggs, separated
85 g (3 oz) caster sugar
55 g (2 oz) ground almonds
40 g (1½ oz) unsalted butter, melted

2 tablespoons Amaretto di Saronno (almond liqueur)
85 g (3 oz) plain chocolate, 70 per cent cocoa solids, broken into pieces
1 tablespoon water

1 Pre-heat the oven to 180°C / 350°F/gas mark 4. Grease and line with greaseproof paper an 18 cm (7 in) round cake tin.

2 Sift the two flours together with the cinnamon. Put the egg yolks in a bowl with the sugar and whisk until light and frothy. Fold in the flours and the almonds, with the melted butter and liqueur.

3 Beat the egg whites until stiff, then carefully fold into the

mixture. Spoon into the prepared tin, and smooth the surface.

4 Bake for about an hour until well risen. Transfer to a wire rack to cool, then turn out of the tin.

5 Melt the chocolate with the water in a bowl over a pan of simmering water. Spread over the cake to cover it completely. Leave until the chocolate has set before serving.

Potato flour gives a magnificent light texture to the cake. Buy it from health-food stores. It consists of the pure starch gathered after soaking grated or pulped potatoes in water, and can be very useful for those forced to eat a gluten-free diet.

ZUCCOTTO

'Little Pumpkin'

This traditional Tuscan dessert is easily recognised by the icing sugar and cocoa with which it is always dusted. It calls for Italian sponge cake which is known as *pan di spagna*. It's like a small pumpkin in shape, thus its name.

SERVES 8

Sponge

butter and flour for greasing
  and dusting
6 free-range eggs,
  separated
150 g (5½ oz) icing sugar,
  sifted
1 teaspoon clear honey
1 teaspoon vanilla extract
85 g (3 oz) potato flour,
  sifted

Filling

85 g (3 oz) shelled almonds,
  toasted and chopped
85 g (3 oz) shelled hazelnuts,
  toasted and chopped
300 g (11 oz) plain chocolate,
  half of it chopped, and
  half melted
1 litre (1¾ pints) whipping
  cream, whipped

To serve

3 tablespoons each of rum,
  brandy and cherry brandy
2 tablespoons each of icing
  sugar and good cocoa
  powder, sifted

1 First make the sponge cake. Butter and flour a 25 cm (10 in) round cake tin. Pre-heat the oven to 190° C / 375° F / gas mark 5.

2 Put the egg yolks in a bowl with the icing sugar, honey and vanilla. Beat energetically with a whisk until foaming and pale yellow. Beat the egg whites until stiff and fold into the egg-yolk mixture. Then sift in the flour and potato flour and fold very delicately into the mixture.

3 Pour into the prepared cake tin and bake for 40 minutes.

Remove from the oven and ease out of the tin on to a wire rack. Leave to cool.

4 Now for the filling. Mix the almonds, hazelnuts and chopped chocolate into the whipped cream. Divide this mixture in half and add the melted chocolate to one half. Chill until required.

5 When the cake is cool, slice the crust off the top and cut the cake in half horizontally. Put one half away to use another time.

6 Brush the sponge with the mixed alcohols until pliable. Place it in a 1.1 litre (2 pint) pudding bowl, and gently ease it down to take the shape of the base of the bowl.

7 Pile in one of the cream mixtures and make smooth, then top with the second cream mixture. Smooth the top. Leave somewhere to soak for about an hour.

8 Invert the set 'pumpkin' on to a serving plate, and dust with icing sugar and cocoa powder.

When you toast nuts, unfortunately you diminish their nutritional value by about a third, but toasting does enhance the flavour of the nuts.

FIORENTINI

Italian Florentines

There are many variations on this luxurious biscuit, which is said to have originated in Austria, despite its Italian-sounding name.

MAKES 8 PIECES

150 g (5½ oz) whole blanched almonds

150 g (5½ oz) whole blanched hazelnuts

225 g (8 oz) natural red glacé cherries

100 g (3½ oz) glacé fruits (eg melon, lemon, orange)

55 g (2 oz) plain flour

½ teaspoon ground allspice

½ teaspoon freshly grated nutmeg

100 g (3½ oz) caster sugar

100 g (3½ oz) clear honey

100 g (3½ oz) plain chocolate

1 Pre-heat the oven to 180° C / 350° F / gas mark 4. Grease a 23 cm (9 in) round cake tin, and line it with baking parchment.

2 Put the almonds and hazelnuts on a baking tray, and toast in the oven for 10 minutes. Put in a mixing bowl, and leave to cool.

3 Wash the cherries, then chop all the fruits and add to the nuts. Sift the flour, allspice and nutmeg over the fruits and nuts, and mix well together.

4 In a saucepan, warm the sugar and honey together over a low heat until the sugar has dissolved. Add the honey mixture to the fruit mixture, and stir together.

5 Turn the mixture into the prepared tin, and level the top. Bake in the oven for 25 minutes, then leave to cool in the tin.

6 Break the chocolate into small pieces and melt in a pan over boiling water. Spread over the nut mixture in an even layer, then, when set, cut into serving pieces.

Buy glacé fruits whole rather than in pieces. These are a real delicacy in Italy, and some of the best glacé fruits come from there. They take ages to prepare, as it's a very delicate operation, so always be prepared to pay much more for them.

TORTA ALLE SUSINE E NOCCIOLE

Warm Plum and Hazelnut Cake

Fresh, juicy plums, which in Italy are ripe in about the middle of September, give this cake a wonderfully moist texture. It is best eaten warm, with a big dollop of double cream or crème fraîche.

SERVES 6

450 g (1 lb) ripe plums
100 g (3½ oz) unsalted butter
85 g (3 oz) soft brown sugar
2 large free-range eggs

225 g (8 oz) self-raising flour
55 g (2 oz) chopped hazelnuts
icing sugar for dusting

1 Preheat the oven to 190°C / 375° F / gas mark 5. Grease and line a 20 cm (8 in) round cake tin.

2 Cut the plums into quarters, discarding the stones.

3 Cream together the butter and sugar until light and fluffy. Then beat in the eggs one at a time, and fold in the flour.

4 Carefully fold in the plums and then pile the mixture into the prepared tin. Sprinkle the hazelnuts on the top, and bake in the oven for 45–50 minutes or until golden brown and firm to the touch.

5 Leave to cool slightly in the tin then turn out and serve slightly warm, dusted with sifted icing sugar.

If fresh plums are not available, you can also use other fruits, such as pears, apples or raspberries, but use only ripe fruit that is in season and bursting with flavour.

TORTA DI CILIEGIA

Succulent Cherry Cake

My great friend in Verona gave me this recipe, which is made to celebrate the new season's cherries in May and June. You have to be quick when harvesting cherries, otherwise the birds get them. There are many varieties, but the best are said to be from Ravenna, near Bologna. Displays of cherries in markets are labelled with their area of origin, and the cherries are also sold in various labelled stages of maturity: ripe, nearly ripe, etc.

SERVES 6

100 g (3½ oz) unsalted butter, softened

150 g (5½ oz) caster sugar

4 free-range eggs, separated

200 g (7 oz) Italian 00 plain flour

1 teaspoon baking powder

1 tablespoon brandy

a pinch of sea salt

675 g (1 lb 6 oz) fresh cherries, washed and pitted

icing sugar for dusting

1 Pre-heat the oven to 180°C / 350°F / gas mark 4. Grease and flour a 20 cm (8 in) cake tin.

2 Cream the butter and sugar together until light and fluffy. Beat the egg yolks with a little of the plain flour. Sieve the remaining flour with the baking powder, and carefully fold into the creamed mixture along with the brandy and egg yolks.

3 Whisk the egg whites with the salt until they stand in stiff peaks. Add 3 teaspoons of the whisked egg white to the creamed mixture and mix well. Fold in the remaining egg white with a metal spoon and carefully spoon into the prepared tin.

4 Scatter the prepared cherries over the top of the cake mixture and press them down lightly. Bake for 35-40 minutes until the cake is well risen and firm to the touch.

5 Allow the cake to cool in the tin, then turn out on to a wire rack and dust with icing sugar.

You can buy cherry stoners, which will stone olives as well. I have many happy memories of sitting under the vines with friends, passatempo, *stoning cherries.*

TORTA DI PESCHE SECCHE E LIMONE

Peach and Lemon Tart

The intensity of the peach works beautifully with the lemon in this recipe, which came from my aunt in Minori. When there is a glut of peaches, in August, she halves them, cuts out the stone, and lays them on a board in the sun, covered with muslin to keep the flies away. The sun is very intense at that time of year, especially at midday, so the peach halves can dry in as short a time as three hours.

SERVES 8

Pastry

225 g (8 oz) Italian 00 plain flour
85 g (3 oz) icing sugar
125 g (4½ oz) unsalted butter
1 large free-range egg
a pinch of sea salt
a few drops of vanilla extract
grated zest of 1 unwaxed lemon

Filling

225 g (8 oz) dried peaches
3 tablespoons water
juice and grated zest of 4 unwaxed lemons
125 g (4½ oz) unsalted butter
1 tablespoon granulated sugar
4 free-range eggs, lightly beaten

1 For the pastry, sift the flour and icing sugar into a bowl, and rub in the butter until the mixture resembles breadcrumbs. Make a well in the centre, and add the egg, salt, vanilla and lemon zest. Gradually work the flour in from the edges and mix to a smooth dough. Wrap in clingfilm and leave to rest in the fridge for about 30 minutes before using.

2 Pre-heat the oven to 200°C/400°F/ gas mark 6.

3 Meanwhile, in a saucepan, boil the dried peaches in the water until they soften: about 20 minutes. Drain and purée the peaches.

4 For the filling, in a bowl over a pan of gently simmering water, combine the lemon juice and zest, butter and sugar. Stir with a wooden spoon until the butter melts. Stir in the eggs, and cook over a medium to low heat until the filling thickens enough to coat the back of the spoon. Be careful not to let the mixture curdle. Remove from the heat and leave to cool.

5 Roll out the pastry to line a 23 cm (9 in) tart tin with a removable base. Bake blind in the pre-heated oven (with greaseproof paper or foil and baking beans) for 10 minutes until nicely golden.

6 Remove the baking beans and paper or foil, and pour the lemon filling into the pastry case. Level the surface then spread over the puréed peaches.

7 Chill for 1 hour, and serve, if you like, with whipped cream.

When fruit is dried, it becomes more intense in flavour, and its nutrients are virtually doubled in the sense of weight: a prune contains more nutrients per 25 g (1 oz) than does the original plum. The sugar content obviously becomes very concentrated as well, but because this is natural, it is not harmful.

BRUTTI MA BUONI

'Bad but Good' Nutty Meringues

In Italy we eat a lot of small cakes or biscuits, particularly after the siesta to give us a burst of energy. Often they are taken to a friend's house, and shared over a cup of coffee and lots of gossip. Wrapped in coloured cellophane, they make wonderful presents.

MAKES ABOUT 18

4 free-range egg whites

55 g (2 oz) vanilla sugar

30 g (1¼ oz) whole almonds, toasted

30 g (1¼ oz) whole hazelnuts, toasted

1 Pre-heat the oven to 110°C / 225°F / gas mark ¼. Line a baking tray with parchment paper.

2 Whisk the egg whites until fluffy, gradually adding the sugar. Never add the sugar all at once as the egg white mixture will collapse.

3 Roughly chop the nuts, and fold them carefully into the meringue mixture.

4 Spoon 2 teaspoons for each meringue on to the parchment-lined tray, and bake in the pre-heated oven for 1½ hours until you get little crisp mounds.

5 Leave to cool, then tuck in, or store in airtight tins.

Vanilla sugar can be made by infusing a vanilla pod in caster sugar. I score the outside of the pod first to release as much of the essential oils as possible. As you use the sugar up, simply add more unflavoured sugar to the container.

TORTA DI MASCARPONE

Lemon Mascarpone Cheesecake

This easy dessert can be served with fresh fruit such as raspberries or strawberries, when they are in season.

SERVES 6–8

85 g (3 oz) unsalted butter

175 g (6 oz) Amaretti biscuits

400 g (14 oz) Mascarpone cheese

grated zest of 3 unwaxed lemons

juice of 1 lemon

100 g (3½ oz) caster sugar

2 free-range eggs, separated

2 tablespoons cornflour

pinch of salt

1 Pre-heat the oven to 180°C / 350°F / gas mark 4.

2 Grease a deep, 20 cm (8 in) loose-bottomed cake tin.

3 Melt the butter. Crush the biscuits, then mix them with the melted butter. Press into the bottom of the greased cake tin.

4 Put the Mascarpone, lemon zest and juice, sugar and egg yolks in a bowl and mix together with a wooden spoon. Sprinkle the cornflour over the top and fold in.

5 In a separate bowl, whisk the egg whites with the salt until stiff. Fold gently into the cheese mixture. Spread the mixture into the cake tin and smooth the top.

6 Bake in the oven for 35 minutes until firm to the touch. Leave to cool in the tin.

This cheesecake can also be made with Ricotta cheese, instead of the Mascarpone.

RICCIARELLI

Tuscan Almond Biscuits

The Sienese version of Amaretti, the perfect *ricciarello* is crisp and powdery on the outside, and tender and moist inside.

MAKES ABOUT 16

175 g (6 oz) whole blanched almonds, or ground almonds

2 medium free-range egg whites

15 g (½ oz) plain flour, sifted

⅓ teaspoon baking powder

125 g (4½ oz) icing sugar, plus extra for rolling and dredging

3 drops almond extract

1 Pre-heat the oven to 220°C/425°F/gas mark 7.

2 If using whole almonds, roast them until golden – a few minutes only – then grind to a powder when they have cooled.

3 Beat the egg whites until they are stiff. Mix the flour and baking powder together, and fold them into the egg whites. Fold in the measured icing sugar, the ground almonds and the almond extract to make a soft paste.

4 Pile some extra icing sugar on to the worktop. For each biscuit, roll a heaped teaspoon of the paste in the icing sugar, then press it into an oblong shape, using the palm of your hand.

5 Place the biscuits well apart from each other on a thoroughly greased baking tray, or they will stick. Bake for 10–12 minutes or until the biscuits are pale and golden and slightly cracked, but with the insides still soft.

6 Remove from the oven and leave to cool on the baking tray. When cold, dredge with more icing sugar.

Using fresh nuts is important for flavour, texture and maximum nutrients. Buy from a reliable source, and look for the date stamp.

BUCCELLATO PALERMITANO

Sweet Fig and Nut Cake

This rich Sicilian fruit and nut tart once more illustrates the Sicilian love of nuts and fruits. Every Sicilian market is full of stalls laden with the local fruits and nuts, and the ground on market days crunches underfoot with shells of the pistachios and pumpkin seeds the stallholders and their customers have enjoyed during the day. I have often thought it is this passion for nuts and seeds, with their Vitamin E content, that makes the skin of Sicilians so healthy and fresh-looking.

SERVES 8

Pastry

150 g (5½ oz) unsalted butter

100 g (3½ oz) caster sugar

300 g (11 oz) Italian 00 plain flour

60 ml (2 fl oz) Marsala

a pinch of sea salt

1 free-range egg yolk

55 g (2 oz) shelled pistachio nuts, finely chopped

icing sugar

Filling

300 g (11 oz) dried figs, chopped

300 g (11 oz) raisins

100 g (3½ oz) shelled almonds, toasted and chopped

55 g (2 oz) shelled walnuts, chopped

grated zest of 2 unwaxed lemons

100 g (3½ oz) plain chocolate, 70 per cent cocoa solids, chopped

60 ml (2 fl oz) Marsala

a pinch of powdered cinnamon

1 For the pastry, work the butter with the sugar and flour in a bowl together with the Marsala and salt. When you have a smooth dough, wrap in clingfilm and leave to rest for an hour.

2 Make the filling by putting all the prepared ingredients into a saucepan. Simmer over a low heat for 20 minutes, stirring frequently. Leave to cool.

3 Pre-heat the oven to 200°C / 400°F / gas mark 6.

4 Using a rolling pin, roll the pastry dough into a rectangle about 1 cm (½ in) thick. Pour the cooked and cooled filling into the centre, roll up the dough, and join the ends to make a ring. Pierce the surface with the tines of a fork, place on a greased baking tray and bake for 25–35 minutes, until golden.

5 Beat the egg yolk. Brush the cake with the yolk, then sprinkle with the chopped pistachio nuts and return to the oven for 5 minutes.

6 Place on a wire rack and leave to cool. Sprinkle with icing sugar and serve.

Marsala is a fortified wine, made in Sicily, and is one of the most famous of Italian wines. There are many types – dry, semi-dry, sweet, gold, amber or ruby – and they are aged in wood for varying times. For this cake, choose an old, dry wine.

TORTA DI MELE D'MARIA
Apple Cake

Maria, who owns San Orsola, where I've spent many happy years teaching, loves this apple cake. The soured cream adds a wonderful acidity to the sweetness of the apple.

SERVES 6–8

1 tablespoon demerara sugar
125 g (4½ oz) unsalted butter
125 g (4½ oz) caster sugar
2 large free-range eggs,
  separated
2 drops pure vanilla extract

125 g (4½ oz) ground almonds
55 g (2 oz) self-raising flour
150 ml (¼ pint) soured cream
175 g (6 oz) Cox's Orange
  Pippin apples
whipped cream to serve

1 Pre-heat the oven to 180°C / 350°F/gas mark 4. Grease and line a 20 cm (8 in) round cake tin with baking parchment, then sprinkle with the demerara sugar.

2 Cream together the butter and caster sugar until light and fluffy. Beat in the egg yolks and vanilla extract, then fold in the almonds, flour and soured cream.

3 Whisk the egg whites until they hold their shape then, using a metal spoon, fold into the creamed mixture.

4 Peel, core and slice the apples, and arrange in the base of the prepared tin. Spoon the creamed mixture over the apples and level the surface. Bake for 45–60 minutes until golden and firm to the touch.

5 Invert on to a warmed serving plate, and serve warm with whipped cream.

Do experiment with other fruits: I've made this cake with soft fruits; with blackberries as well as apple when there was a glut of both; and with plums. The plums were fantastic!

PANFORTE DI SIENA

'Strong Bread'

This flat sweet cake, which has a nougat-like texture, is rich in candied peel, toasted nuts and spices, and is a speciality of Siena, dating from the twelfth century. There are many variations, but this is my favourite, and is said to be the original. There is a shop in Siena called Nannini which sells at least fifteen different varieties of *panforte*; you can mix and match to decide which you like the best!

SERVES ABOUT 10

85 g (3 oz) shelled hazelnuts

85 g (3 oz) blanched almonds, coarsely chopped

175 g (6 oz) candied peel, finely chopped

25 g (1 oz) cocoa powder

55 g (2 oz) plain flour

½ teaspoons powdered cinnamon

¼ teaspoon ground mixed spice

100 g (3½ oz) caster sugar

100 g (3½ oz) clear honey

Topping

2 tablespoons icing sugar

1 teaspoon powdered cinnamon

1 Pre-heat the oven to 150°C / 300°F / gas mark 2.

2 Place the nuts in a bowl with the candied peel, cocoa, flour and spices and stir well.

3 Put the sugar and honey in a pan and heat gently until a sugar thermometer registers about 115°C / 240°F, or until a little of the mixture dropped into a cup of water forms a ball. Take off the heat immediately, add to the nut mixture and stir to mix well.

4 Turn into a 20 cm (8 in) flan ring lined with non-stick parchment. Spread flat, making sure that the mixture is no more than 1 cm (½ in) thick.

5 Bake in the pre-heated oven for 30 minutes. Turn on to a wire rack, peel off the paper and leave to cool.

6 Sprinkle the top thickly with icing sugar and cinnamon. Cut into small wedges.

The cake is said to have been devised during the Italian Crusades as something to give strength and energy, since nuts and seeds, the cocoa and honey are all storehouses of energy-giving nutrients.

NEPITELLA

Fig and Nut Pastries

I can't think of a nicer combination than figs and walnuts. Both are really health- and energy-giving foods. Eat these little half-moon or *mezzaluna* pastries with coffee or after a siesta, never after lunch as a dessert.

MAKES ABOUT 14

400 g (14 oz) Italian 00 plain
    flour
150 g (5½ oz) caster sugar
150 g (5½ oz) butter, softened
    and cut into small pieces
3 free-range eggs, 1 of them
    separated
a pinch of sea salt

Filling
300 g (11 oz) dried figs
150 g (5½ oz) walnuts, ground

150 g (5½ oz) blanched
    almonds, toasted and ground
100 g (3½ oz) seedless raisins,
    soaked in lukewarm water for
    15 minutes and drained
200 g (7 oz) marmalade
finely grated rind of 3
    unwaxed oranges
¼ teaspoon ground cloves
1 teaspon powdered cinnamon

1 Pre-heat the oven to 170°C /
325°F / gas mark 3.

2 To make the pastry, sift the flour into a bowl, stir in the sugar then make a well in the centre. Add the butter, 2 eggs, the separated egg yolk and the salt. Work the ingredients together with the fingertips to form a soft dough, then knead well until smooth and elastic. Shape the dough into a ball, cover and chill.

3 Cook the figs in boiling water for 10 minutes. Drain thoroughly, cool, then chop. Place in a bowl with the remaining filling ingredients and mix well.

4 Take the dough and, with a rolling pin, roll out to a sheet about 5 mm (¼ in) thick. Cut into 10 cm (4 in) circles, using a pastry cutter.

5 Put a little filling in the middle of each circle then fold the dough over to form a half-moon shape. Moisten the edges with beaten egg white then press firmly to seal. Make a few cuts in the top of each pastry. Place on a greased baking sheet.

6 Bake in the pre-heated oven for 25–35 minutes until golden. Serve hot or cold.

Nuts are a rich source of unsaturated oil and protein: almonds contain 40–60 per cent of the former, 20 per cent of the latter; walnuts 70 and 15 per cent respectively.

THE ITALIAN
STORECUPBOARD

A WELL-STOCKED STORECUPBOARD, refrigerator and freezer not only save you endless shopping trips but also mean you are able to make a nutritious meal at a moment's notice. The following are the ingredients that I consider essential.

Pasta and Grains Grains of all sorts are a useful source in the vegetarian diet of protein and carbohydrate. Pasta is made from wheat, and I keep a large variety of dried pasta in various shapes and sizes. It should be an integral part of our lives, being economical, nutritious, quick to prepare, versatile and filling. When buying pasta, check on the packet that it is made from 100 per cent durum wheat or states *semola di grano*. When it contains egg it will also state *all'uovo*. Choice is very much personal taste but as a general rule, use thin pasta for fairly thick sauces, hollow or twisted shapes for chunky sauces, wide flat noodles for rich sauces and delicate shapes for light sauces. There are a variety of tiny shapes which are useful for soups. When buying pasta, check the date marking and store in airtight containers in a cool dark place.

Other useful grain foods are Italian 00 plain flour for making fresh pasta; strong white unbleached flour for bread-making; plain white flour for cakes, pastries and sauces; *arborio*, *carnaroli* and *vialone nano* rices for risotto; pot barley; semolina.

Pulses Pulses are the 'seeds' of plants, and so are rich in nutrients, particularly slow-release carbohydrate and vegetable protein. Those I use most include cannellini, haricot and borlotti beans (preferably dried); chick peas (and chick-pea flour); green lentils.

Nuts and Seeds A very rich source of natural fats and proteins for vegetarians. The ones I like best are hazelnuts; pine kernels; ground, flaked and blanched whole almonds; pistachio nuts; walnuts; chestnuts (dried); sesame seeds; pumpkin seeds; aniseed seeds; sunflower seeds. (Store in the refrigerator or freezer to preserve their Vitamin E content.)

Dried Fruits Concentrated goodness! If possible choose those not preserved with sulphur dioxide as they have more flavour and nutritional value: apricots; prunes; figs; pears; peaches; raisins; sultanas; glacé cherries; candied fruit.

Oils Cold-pressed olive oil, which is monounsaturated, is thought to contribute in a very positive way to the diet. Choose extra-virgin olive oil for dressings and sprinkling, olive oil for frying.

Cans Tomatoes (whole Italian plum, and chopped); different sorts of beans, chick peas, lentils (if you haven't time to soak dried).

Bottles and Jars Balsamic vinegar; red- and white-wine vinegar; green and black olives; capers (bottled in brine or vinegar, and salted); sun-dried tomatoes; passata (sieved tomatoes); gherkins; natural vanilla and almond extracts; honey; jams and preserves; red and white wine; a selection of spirits and liqueurs.

Herbs Fresh herbs have a much better, truer flavour than dried herbs, and their nutritional benefits, contained in their essential oils, are still intact. Most can be easily grown on a windowsill, inside or out, or in the garden. Keep some dried or frozen herbs such as bay leaves, rosemary, oregano, sage and thyme for emergencies. Garlic, although not a herb but a member of the onion family, is used as a flavouring ingredient in the same way as fresh herbs. It will keep in a cool place for about six weeks.

Spices Whole fresh spices have a better flavour than bought ground. Buy whole spices and grind them yourself or, if buying ground or powdered, do so in small quantities, and use them up quickly as the essential oils which provide the flavour are lost. Spices I find invaluable are whole nutmeg; whole and powdered cinnamon and cloves (these are difficult to grind at home); powdered saffron; dried chilli-pepper flakes; ground allspice and mixed

spice; and fennel seeds. I also could not cook without sea salt (coarse and flake varieties) and whole black peppercorns. For good flavour I use the small fresh chilli (*peperoncino*).

Dairy Products   These are a vital source of protein and fat for vegetarians. Such 'storecupboard' ingredients are, of course, perishable and should therefore be stored in the refrigerator: free-range eggs, milk, single and double cream, soured cream, unsalted butter, and cheeses.

Parmesan, the king of Italian cheese, is irreplaceable in Italian cooking: choose the expensive *Parmigiano Reggiano* or the slightly cheaper (because less matured) *Grana Padano*. Other Italian cheeses I find very useful in various dishes are Pecorino, Fontina, Mozzarella, Dolcelatte, Gorgonzola, Ricotta and Mascarpone.

Cheeses are usually made with animal rennet and are therefore not suitable for the strict vegetarian. However, the range of cheeses available made with vegetable rennet – including Parmesan – is increasing, so look out for them if this is important to you.

Miscellaneous   Fresh and dried yeast; packets of dried *porcini* (*Boletus edulis,* cep or wild mushroom); plain chocolate; sugars (keep a vanilla pod in caster for vanilla sugar); baking powder; cocoa powder; potato flour.

221

Klasmann Potgrond
Gemüsejungpflanzen mit edle Pflanzen zur Anzucht von
anteil erhöht die Kulturdauer. Der Weißtorf
Wurzelwachstum, und optimiert das

Die physikali und chemischen Eigenschaf
neben der Jungpflanzen. Die
Wek Mär ofdüng
stoffe burg

INDEX

ACKNOWLEDGEMENTS

What a joy to write this book and have the finest support available to make it happen.

Special thanks must go to my editor Susan Fleming for her constant good spirits and dedicated hard work. I had such fun with her and lots of giggles during the summer of 1998; to Margaret Little for shaping, developing and overseeing the whole project with gentle guidance and calm and for her ability to make the book stand out in the crowd; to Gaye Allen for her splendid designer's eye in ensuring the book looks so great, and for her kindness, gentleness and dedication throughout – working with you in Italy was wonderful; and to Jason Lowe for his exceptional photography – I adore the way in which he works, it was so inspiring and determined.